Independent Task Force Report No. 79

China's Belt and Road

Implications for the United States

Jacob J. Lew and Gary Roughead, *Chairs*
Jennifer Hillman and David Sacks, *Project Directors*

The Council on Foreign Relations (CFR) is an independent, nonpartisan membership organization, think tank, and publisher dedicated to being a resource for its members, government officials, business executives, journalists, educators and students, civic and religious leaders, and other interested citizens in order to help them better understand the world and the foreign policy choices facing the United States and other countries. Founded in 1921, CFR carries out its mission by maintaining a diverse membership, with special programs to promote interest and develop expertise in the next generation of foreign policy leaders; convening meetings at its headquarters in New York and in Washington, DC, and other cities where senior government officials, members of Congress, global leaders, and prominent thinkers come together with Council members to discuss and debate major international issues; supporting a Studies Program that fosters independent research, enabling CFR scholars to produce articles, reports, and books and hold roundtables that analyze foreign policy issues and make concrete policy recommendations; publishing *Foreign Affairs*, the preeminent journal on international affairs and U.S. foreign policy; sponsoring Independent Task Forces that produce reports with both findings and policy prescriptions on the most important foreign policy topics; and providing up-to-date information and analysis about world events and American foreign policy on its website, CFR.org.

The Council on Foreign Relations takes no institutional positions on policy issues and has no affiliation with the U.S. government. All views expressed in its publications and on its website are the sole responsibility of the author or authors.

The Council on Foreign Relations sponsors Independent Task Forces to assess issues of current and critical importance to U.S. foreign policy and provide policymakers with concrete judgments and recommendations. Diverse in backgrounds and perspectives, Task Force members aim to reach a meaningful consensus on policy through private deliberations. Once launched, Task Forces are independent of CFR and solely responsible for the content of their reports. Task Force members are asked to join a consensus signifying that they endorse "the general policy thrust and judgments reached by the group, though not necessarily every finding and recommendation." Each Task Force member also has the option of putting forward an additional or a dissenting view. Members' affiliations are listed for identification purposes only and do not imply institutional endorsement. Task Force observers participate in discussions, but are not asked to join the consensus.

For further information about CFR or this Task Force, please write to the Council on Foreign Relations, 58 East 68th Street, New York, NY 10065, or call the Communications office at 212.434.9888. Visit our website, CFR.org.

TASK FORCE MEMBERS

Task Force members are asked to join a consensus signifying that they endorse "the general policy thrust and judgments reached by the group, though not necessarily every finding and recommendation." They participate in the Task Force in their individual, not institutional, capacities.

B. Marc Allen

Charlene Barshefsky
WilmerHale

Brendan P. Bechtel
Bechtel Group, Inc.

Charles Boustany Jr.
Capitol Counsel, LLC

L. Reginald Brothers Jr.
NuWave Solutions

Joyce Chang
JPMorgan Chase & Co.

Evan A. Feigenbaum
Carnegie Endowment for International Peace

Jennifer Hillman
Council on Foreign Relations

Christopher M. Kirchhoff
Schmidt Futures

Jacob J. Lew
Columbia University's School of International and Public Affairs

Natalie Lichtenstein
Johns Hopkins University's School of Advanced International Studies

Gary Locke
Bellevue College

Oriana Skylar Mastro
Freeman Spogli Institute for International Studies, Stanford University

Daniel H. Rosen
Rhodium Group

Gary Roughead
Hoover Institution, Stanford University

David Sacks
Council on Foreign Relations

Nadia Schadlow
Hudson Institute

Rajiv J. Shah
Rockefeller Foundation

Kristen Silverberg
Business Roundtable

Taiya M. Smith
Climate Leadership Council

Susan A. Thornton
Yale Law School

Ramin Toloui
Stanford University

Macani Toungara

Frederick H. Tsai
Liferay

CONTENTS

FOREWORD

Faced with a China that is more repressive at home and more assertive abroad, there is bipartisan support in the United States for a tougher approach to China. This is likely to endure for the foreseeable future. There are, however, competing views regarding China's ultimate goals and intentions. To some, China is a revisionist power seeking to displace the United States and build a Sinocentric world order and therefore should be countered at every step. Others assess China's goal as establishing its primacy throughout the Asia-Pacific, while to some China has more limited objectives, largely confined to extending the government's writ to all territory (including Taiwan) it sees as Chinese.

Studying China's Belt and Road Initiative (BRI) is critical to understanding Beijing's intentions and capabilities. BRI is Chinese President Xi Jinping's signature foreign policy endeavor and the largest ever global infrastructure undertaking, far surpassing the Marshall Plan. Under the auspices of BRI, Chinese banks and companies have devoted billions of dollars to funding and building roads, power plants, railways, ports, and telecommunications infrastructure in dozens of countries.

To some analysts, BRI is China's primary conduit for pursuing global domination. This Task Force, however, argues that China pursued BRI primarily to address a number of domestic issues, such as closing the gap between the country's affluent coastal cities and its impoverished interior, absorbing excess manufacturing capacity, putting its accumulated savings to use, and securing inputs for its manufacturing sector. Much of Chinese foreign policy is animated by a drive to bolster domestic political stability, which in turn relies on steady economic growth, and BRI is no exception.

Although BRI constitutes a prominent element of Chinese foreign policy, the initiative remains remarkably opaque. BRI has no central governing institution. China has not published a master list of BRI projects, the terms of which are often negotiated behind closed doors and kept secret. When projects run into trouble, Beijing often pressures countries to keep all renegotiations private.

This Task Force has done much to peel back the curtain, analyzing what is known about BRI and piecing together a comprehensive view of the initiative. The Task Force finds that BRI worryingly adds to countries' debt burdens, locks countries into carbon-intensive futures, tilts the playing field in major markets toward Chinese companies, and draws countries into tighter economic and political relationships with Beijing. It concludes that "the risks for both the United States and recipient countries raised by BRI's implementation considerably outweigh its benefits."

The Task Force assesses that BRI poses a significant challenge to U.S. interests, as it has the potential to displace American companies from BRI countries, set technical standards that are incompatible with U.S. products, push countries to politically align with China, and pressure countries to withhold access to U.S. forces during a potential crisis.

The Task Force also looks at how the COVID-19 pandemic is reshaping BRI, providing one of the first comprehensive analyses of BRI in a COVID and post-COVID world. The Task Force argues that the pandemic "has revealed the flaws of China's BRI model, forcing a reckoning with concerns that many BRI projects are not economically viable and elevating questions of debt sustainability." BRI is likely to emerge from the pandemic as a more slimmed-down, cost-effective, and technology-focused undertaking, but it is not going away.

The pandemic has made a U.S. response to BRI all the more essential and urgent. The Task Force proposes a response that rests on four pillars: mitigating the economic risks of BRI, improving U.S. competitiveness, strengthening the multilateral response to BRI, and protecting U.S. security interests in BRI countries. The report asserts that the United States should focus on those areas where it can offer a genuine alternative to BRI and puts forward an array of sensible policy prescriptions that the Biden administration would be wise to adopt.

It is clear that the United States can only protect its interests and compete with BRI if it gets its own house in order. The Task Force emphasizes that a response to BRI should begin at home by increasing funding for federal research and development; boosting investment in basic science, technology, engineering, and mathematics (STEM) education; amending immigration and visa policies; promoting U.S. digital transformation alternatives to the developing world; and reforming the Development Finance Corporation and the Export-Import Bank of the United States. A United States beset by internal problems that is unable to both compete and set an example will be unable to offer an alternative to BRI.

In addition, the United States can and should use its leadership role in institutions such as the World Bank to offer an economically sustainable and green alternative to BRI. America's unprecedented network of allies and partners allows it to pool resources to offer choices in the developing world—something China cannot do. While the Donald J. Trump administration spent the last four years deriding the post–World War II order, this report demonstrates how important it remains for U.S. foreign policy.

Finally, despite its flaws, BRI has filled a void left by the United States and its allies. BRI thus demonstrates how U.S. interests suffer when our country unwisely withdraws from important areas of the world and how essential it is that the United States reassert its leadership. If the United States ends up as a bystander as China leverages BRI to draw countries firmly into its orbit, it can expect a world in which U.S. companies have to compete on unfair terms, trade networks are geared toward China, debt levels and carbon-intensive power continue to rise in the developing world, and countries become more politically beholden to China. The good news is the Task Force provides a blueprint for avoiding such a future.

I would like to thank the Task Force chairs, Jacob J. Lew and Gary Roughead, for their significant contributions to this important project. My thanks extend to all the Task Force members and observers for lending their knowledge and experience. This report would not have been possible without CFR's Jennifer Hillman and David Sacks, who directed the Task Force and authored this report, and Independent Task Force Program Director Anya Schmemann, who guided this project. They have all earned our thanks for taking on such a difficult but important topic.

Richard N. Haass
President
Council on Foreign Relations
March 2021

ACKNOWLEDGMENTS

This Independent Task Force report is the result of the dedication and collaboration of a diverse group of experts committed to understanding China's global ambitions and how the United States should respond. We are grateful to the Task Force members and observers for their attention, guidance, and feedback over the course of this project. We want to thank former CFR Fellow Mira Rapp-Hooper, whose important work as the initial Task Force project director set this endeavor on an excellent path.

We would especially like to thank our Task Force co-chairs Jack Lew and Gary Roughead for lending their knowledge, experience, editorial skills, and leadership to this project. Their insights and guidance strengthened the report at every turn, and it was a privilege to work with them.

Our gratitude extends to those who provided briefings and shared their time and expertise. We were fortunate to have the opportunity to exchange views with a number of experts who have worked inside the U.S. government and with other institutions dedicated to understanding and responding to BRI. In particular, we would like to thank David Bohigian, David Bradley, Kendra Brock, Joshua Cartin, David Feith, Benjamin Frohman, Charles Horne, Isaac Kardon, Agatha Kratz, Sigal Mandelker, Jason Matheny, Matthew Mingey, Leyton Nelson, Matthew Pottinger, Emma Rafaelof, Nargiza Salidjanova, Suzanna Stephens, and David Trulio.

Our CFR colleagues who served as Task Force observers—Paul Angelo, Alyssa Ayres, Michelle Gavin, Joshua Kurlantzick, Mira Rapp-Hooper, and Benn Steil—provided invaluable feedback on earlier drafts. Other CFR experts, including Elizabeth Economy, Alice Hill, Yanzhong Huang, Robert Knake, and Adam Segal, generously reviewed this report. Although we sought the advice of many, we are ultimately responsible for the final content of this report.

This report would not be possible without the support of many at CFR. We thank the Publications team for copyediting and preparing the report for publication. The Digital Product and Design team deserves recognition for designing and producing the excellent maps and graphics that appear in this report. We want to thank Callie McQuilkin, who dug through dozens of sources to create datasets for multiple graphics and helped tame our endnotes. Our gratitude extends to Max Yoeli, who provided research on BRI's economic consequences and deftly analyzed BRI projects in Kenya. And we are grateful to Kirk Lancaster for his research support in the early stages of this project.

We are especially grateful to Anya Schmemann, who guided this project from inception to report launch despite the many disruptions brought on by the coronavirus pandemic. And to Chelie Setzer and Sara Shah, who provided invaluable support by organizing meetings, editing drafts, and coordinating with various CFR departments to produce and promote the report—thank you. Finally, we thank CFR President Richard N. Haass for identifying BRI as an important topic deserving of a Task Force's attention and for giving us the opportunity to coauthor this report.

Jennifer Hillman
David Sacks

Project Directors

*INDEPENDENT
TASK FORCE REPORT*

EXECUTIVE SUMMARY

The Belt and Road Initiative (BRI), Chinese President Xi Jinping's signature foreign policy undertaking and the world's largest infrastructure program, poses a significant challenge to U.S. economic, political, climate change, security, and global health interests. Since BRI's launch in 2013, Chinese banks and companies have financed and built everything from power plants, railways, highways, and ports to telecommunications infrastructure, fiber-optic cables, and smart cities around the world. If implemented sustainably and responsibly, BRI has the potential to meet long-standing developing country needs and spur global economic growth. To date, however, the risks for both the United States and recipient countries raised by BRI's implementation considerably outweigh its benefits.

BRI was initially designed to connect China's modern coastal cities to its underdeveloped interior and to its Southeast, Central, and South Asian neighbors, cementing China's position at the center of a more connected world. The initiative has since outgrown its original regional corridors, expanding to all corners of the globe. Its scope now includes a Digital Silk Road intended to improve recipients' telecommunications networks, artificial intelligence capabilities, cloud computing, e-commerce and mobile payment systems, surveillance technology, and other high-tech areas, along with a Health Silk Road designed to operationalize China's vision of global health governance.[1] Hundreds of projects around the world now fall under the BRI umbrella.

China pursued BRI out of a belief that the initiative could simultaneously address a number of issues, including

- closing the gap between the country's affluent coastal cities and its impoverished interior, thus boosting domestic political stability;

- absorbing its excess manufacturing capacity;

- putting its accumulated savings to work;

- securing a consistent source of inputs for its manufacturing sector; and

- reorienting global commerce away from the United States and Western Europe toward China.

The Task Force finds that China is advancing this initiative in worrying ways that

- undermine global macroeconomic stability and increase the likelihood that debt crises will materialize over the coming years by largely eschewing debt sustainability analysis and funding economically questionable projects in heavily indebted countries;

- subsidize privileged market entry for state-owned and non–market oriented Chinese companies;

- enable China to lock countries in to Chinese ecosystems by pressing its technology and preferred technical standards on BRI recipients;

- ensure countries' dependence on carbon-intensive power for decades through its export of coal-fired power plants, making climate change mitigation significantly more difficult;

- make it harder for the World Bank and other traditional lenders to insist on high standards by offering quick and easy infrastructure packages that forego rigorous environmental- and social-impact assessments, ignoring project management best practices and tolerating corruption; and

- leave countries more susceptible to Chinese political pressure while giving China a greater ability to project its power more widely.

U.S. inaction as much as Chinese assertiveness is responsible for the economic and strategic predicament in which the United States finds itself. U.S. withdrawal helped create the vacuum that China filled with BRI. Although the United States long ago identified an interest in promoting infrastructure, trade, and connectivity throughout Asia and repeatedly invoked the imagery of the Silk Road, it has not met the inherent needs of the region.[2] Its own lending to and investment in many BRI countries was limited and is now declining. Its cutbacks in research and development and investments in advanced technologies have allowed China to move ahead in the development and sale of fifth-generation (5G) technology, the installation of high-speed rail, the production of solar and wind energy, the promulgation of electronic payment platforms, the development of ultra-high-voltage transmission systems, and more. Despite enjoying a leading role in the World Bank and regional development banks, the United States has watched those institutions move away from backing significant infrastructure projects. Washington has not joined regional trade and investment agreements that would have enhanced U.S. economic ties to Asia.

These collective shortcomings allowed China to tap into a legitimate need around the world for new infrastructure and to fill the gap in infrastructure financing and construction in a way that benefits it. Beijing's ability to offer hard and digital infrastructure around the world at low prices is made possible by a combination of political backing from the Chinese Communist Party, the financial power of its state-owned banks, excess capacity in a number of important sectors, and its development of large, highly capable manufacturing and technology companies. If BRI meets little competition or resistance, Beijing could become the hub of global trade, set important technical standards that would disadvantage non-Chinese companies, lock countries into carbon-intensive power generation, have greater influence over countries' political decisions, and acquire more power-projection capabilities for its military.

The United States has a clear interest in adopting a strategy that both pressures China to alter its BRI practices and provides an effective alternative to BRI—one that promotes sustainable infrastructure, upholds high environmental and anticorruption standards, ensures U.S. companies can operate on a level playing field, and assists countries in preserving their political independence.

To do so, the Task Force recommends a four-pronged strategy: address specific economic risks posed by BRI; improve U.S. competitiveness; work with allies, partners, and multilateral organizations to better meet developing countries' needs; and act to protect U.S. security interests in BRI countries. The United States cannot and should not respond to BRI symmetrically, attempting to match China dollar for dollar or project for project. Instead, the United States should focus on those areas where it can offer, either on its own or in concert with like-minded nations, a compelling alternative to BRI. Such an alternative would leverage core U.S. strengths, including cutting-edge technologies, world-class companies, deep pools of capital, a history of international leadership, a traditional role in setting international standards, and support for the rule of law and transparent business practices.

To mitigate the economic risks of BRI, the Task Force recommends

- leading a global effort to address emerging BRI-induced debt crises and to promote adherence to high-standards lending practices;

- enhancing U.S. commercial diplomacy to promote U.S. high-quality, high-standards alternatives to BRI and to raise public awareness in host countries of the environmental and economic costs of certain BRI projects;

- offering technical support to BRI countries to help them vet prospective projects for economic and environmental sustainability; and

- embarking on a robust anticorruption campaign.

To improve U.S. competitiveness, the Task Force recommends

- devoting an additional $100 billion toward federal research and development funding, with further investments in universities and research institutions to fund cutting-edge research, and enhanced support for private-sector investment in next-generation technologies;

- increasing investment in basic science, technology, engineering, and mathematics (STEM) education at all levels;

- amending immigration and visa policies to make it easier to attract and retain the world's brightest students, researchers, scientists, and engineers;

- improving coordination and providing greater support for participation in international standards-setting bodies;

- reforming the Development Finance Corporation and the Export-Import Bank of the United States by providing them with greater flexibility to compete with BRI's offerings and to partner with other development finance institutions from around the world; and

- promoting U.S. digital transformation alternatives to the developing world.

To strengthen the multilateral response to BRI, the Task Force recommends

- working with allies and partners to reenergize the World Bank so that it can offer a better alternative to BRI;

- negotiating sectoral trade agreements with important regional partners, starting with digital trade agreements, and working to improve and then join the Comprehensive and Progressive Agreement for Trans-Pacific Partnership; and

- insisting that China live up to its pledges for a green belt and road by requiring pre-project environmental assessments, denying financing or insurance to projects likely to have significant adverse environmental effects, and adopting binding standards for what constitutes a green BRI investment.

To protect U.S. security interests in BRI countries, the Task Force recommends

- creating mitigation plans for possible Chinese disruption of critical infrastructure in BRI countries;

- investing in undersea cables and undersea cable security; and

- training cyber diplomats who can work with host governments to reduce cyber vulnerabilities.

The COVID-19 pandemic has made a U.S. response to BRI all the more needed and urgent. The global economic contraction has revealed the flaws of China's BRI model, forcing a reckoning with concerns that many BRI projects are not economically viable and elevating questions of debt sustainability. Unless BRI-related debt is addressed, countries that are already being battered by the COVID-19 pandemic could be forced to choose between making debt payments and providing health-care and other social services to their citizens.

INTRODUCTION

In the fall of 2013, shortly after assuming power, Chinese President Xi Jinping proposed building a land-based "Silk Road Economic Belt," extending from China to Central and South Asia, the Middle East, and Europe, and a sea-based "21st Century Maritime Silk Road," connecting China to Southeast Asia, the Middle East, Africa, and Europe via major sea lanes (see figure 1). Together, these would form the Belt and Road Initiative (BRI), still known officially in Chinese as "One Belt, One Road," which Xi labeled "a project of the century" and which quickly became his signature foreign policy undertaking.[3]

Chinese leaders have long sought to close the gap between the country's booming coastal cities and its impoverished interior and to absorb excess capacity in some sectors by promoting connectivity between southwestern and western regions of China and Southeast, Central, and South Asia. BRI is, in many ways, the latest in a succession of plans to do this.[4] In the seven-plus years since Xi introduced BRI, China has funded and built a vast array of roads, railways, power plants, ports, smart cities, telecommunications, and information technology and e-commerce platforms around the world. It has promoted people-to-people ties, financial integration, and closer trade relationships with a range of other countries under the banner of BRI. In so doing, China is both meeting the needs of many in the developing world and filling a void left by the United States, its allies, and the multilateral development banks.

The initiative has since outgrown the original corridors outlined by Xi and become a globe-spanning enterprise encompassing 139 countries (although not every country that has formally signed on to BRI hosts BRI projects), with Latin America added as a "natural extension of the 21st Century Maritime Silk Road."[5] BRI's scope has also grown, becoming a more amorphous undertaking, with China adding a Digital Silk Road (DSR), Health Silk Road (HSR), and Green Belt and Road, which are unbounded geographically.

Chinese officials insist BRI's main objective is to spur development in participating countries, while acknowledging its additional contribution to China's economic growth. They disavow any strategic rationale behind BRI, with Xi stating China "will not resort to outdated geopolitical maneuvering" while pursuing the initiative.[6] Xi further has said that BRI is "an initiative for economic cooperation, instead of a geopolitical alliance or military league" and that China does not "play the zero-sum game."[7] The Chinese government objects to any comparison between BRI and the Marshall Plan because the latter had a geostrategic angle.[8]

BRI, if implemented sustainably, has the potential to bolster economic growth in the developing world, but it was never a straightforward altruistic endeavor. Instead, BRI is designed to advance an array of Chinese economic, political, and geopolitical interests while filling a vital need in many countries for reliable sources of power and better infrastructure.[9] China spent hundreds of billions of dollars on economic stimulus following the 2008 global financial crisis but witnessed diminishing returns on its investments. Not wanting to shrink the size of its state-owned enterprises (SOEs), China is seeking to export its excess manufacturing capacity while putting its accumulated savings to work in BRI countries. China also has the ability, through BRI, to secure cheap inputs for its manufacturing sector and set technical standards in foreign countries that could give its companies a leg up in those markets.

Figure 1. THE ORIGINAL VISION OF THE BELT AND
ROAD INITIATIVE WAS MORE LIMITED

— Silk Road Economic Belt   — Maritime Silk Road

For more detailed versions of the graphics in this report, including tables with BRI projects, visit
www.cfr.org/BeltAndRoad.

Sources: Xinhua; CFR research.

China's leaders hope the new trade routes and more efficient
transportation networks created by BRI will reorient global commerce
away from the United States and Western Europe toward China.
They believe BRI has the potential to increase economic growth in
China's underdeveloped and often restive southwestern and western
provinces, thus boosting domestic political stability. By becoming a
major creditor to the developing world, China is accruing leverage
that potentially enables it to exert pressure on BRI countries to not
challenge its position on strategic issues, human rights, or Chinese
domestic politics. And BRI allows China to acquire global intelligence
capabilities and access to overseas ports and other facilities that it likely
hopes to use in the future to project military power.

The COVID-19 pandemic has upended BRI and complicated
implementation, slowing the flow of Chinese labor and supplies to
foreign countries, eviscerating host countries' abilities to pay for
projects, and forcing countries to stall or cancel expensive projects.[10]
In addition, in the years since BRI was introduced, China's current

account surplus and its foreign exchange reserves have shrunk, in part because of Beijing's macroeconomic adjustments. China no longer has the same financial cushion that it once enjoyed, and with many projects postponed or canceled, Chinese banks have begun to increase their scrutiny of BRI projects, with lending slowing substantially from its 2017 peak.[11] Indeed, Chinese banks and firms are becoming more methodical and risk-averse in their approach to BRI projects.[12]

BRI is likely to become a more slimmed-down, cost-effective, and technology-focused undertaking. But the initiative is not going away. With BRI now enshrined in the Chinese Communist Party's (CCP) constitution and Xi Jinping set to rule China indefinitely, Xi's trademark initiative will certainly continue, repurposed for the pandemic and post-pandemic world.

Background

Xi has cast BRI as an effort to reconstitute the ancient Silk Road, a series of trade networks that connected China to modern-day South and Central Asia and later extended to parts of Europe and Africa.[13] He proposed updating these trade routes for the twenty-first century by investing as much as $1 trillion in building infrastructure in dozens of countries. Just as the ancient Silk Road centered on China, so, too, would its modern equivalent, with projects facilitating trade and investment with China and connecting the country with emerging economies around the world. With a successful BRI, China would cement its position as the region's economic and political center of gravity.

Many developing countries were initially eager to embrace the concept and receive BRI funding, revealing that China had identified a significant gap between global demand for infrastructure and the record of existing institutions in meeting that demand. In countries alongside BRI corridors, both trade and foreign direct investment (FDI) are estimated to be lower than potential, by 30 percent and 70 percent, respectively, because of poor integration and connectivity.[14] The World Bank estimates that $97 trillion needs to be spent on infrastructure globally by 2040 in order to maintain economic growth and to meet the UN Sustainable Development Goals, but an $18 trillion gap exists.[15] Asia alone is expected to require $26 trillion in infrastructure investments by 2030 to maintain growth and respond to climate change.[16] Latin America and the Caribbean need an additional $120 to 150 billion per year in investment to close their infrastructure gap.[17]

Despite these significant needs, multilateral development banks (MDBs) and traditional donors were devoting a growing share of their funding to social services, opening the door to China to fund hard infrastructure projects. Moreover, multilateral lenders insist that their projects meet environmental and other sustainability standards not demanded by Beijing, making it easier for China to initiate infrastructure projects. As a result, Chinese lending to infrastructure projects in developing countries now far exceeds that of comparable lending by all major MDBs combined.[18]

Xi set the broad contours of BRI, but it was never institutionalized into a coherent or coordinated enterprise; no obvious BRI master plan is in place. BRI has no central governing institution, and instead numerous actors shape the initiative, including policy banks, SOEs, China's National Development and Reform Commission (NDRC), its Ministry of Commerce (MOFCOM), and its Ministry of Foreign Affairs (MFA), all of which have their own priorities and interests and often do not coordinate with one another.[19] Most projects take shape through a bottom-up approach and are approved on a case-by-case basis, with the recipient government creating a wish list, often in consultation with Chinese SOEs, and presenting it to MOFCOM and the NDRC for funding.[20] BRI is adaptive and responsive to demand pulls: it expanded into Latin America not primarily at the behest of Chinese officials but rather because of lobbying by Latin American political elites.[21]

The central government in Beijing does not have the capacity to keep track of the implementation of hundreds of projects scattered across the world.[22] The lack of centralized governance and oversight has allowed corruption and rent-seeking behavior to flourish in projects in a number of BRI countries, providing an opening for local political elites to distort legitimate infrastructure needs for their own gain and

Figure 2. THE BELT AND ROAD INITIATIVE HAS GONE GLOBAL

Official BRI participants by year of joining

● 2013–14   ● 2015–16   ● 2017–18   ● 2019 or later   ○ Unknown

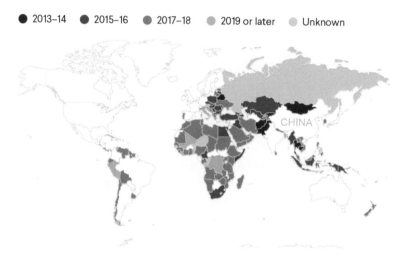

Sources: Green Belt and Road Initiative Center; Belt and Road Portal.

for the gain of Chinese producers of goods and services. BRI is, in many ways, more of a Chinese branding exercise than an institution.

China has not publicly disclosed the exact number of projects underway or the full scope of the initiative, leading to greatly varying estimates of BRI's size. The initiative's scope could also be purposefully vague, allowing the CCP to claim only its successes and disassociate BRI from failures while redefining its objectives over time, as it has begun to do during the COVID-19 crisis. SOEs and private firms in China have been adept at getting non-BRI projects rebranded as BRI ones to garner additional political backing for them.[23]

BRI seeks to back an array of projects, but to date, the vast majority of funds have been allocated toward traditional infrastructure— energy, roads, railways, and ports.[24] Though principally aimed at developing countries, with Pakistan, Malaysia, Bangladesh, Myanmar, and Sri Lanka among the largest recipients of BRI funds, BRI also includes developed countries, with numerous U.S. allies participating (see figure 2).[25] If these U.S. allies were to turn to BRI to build critical infrastructure, such as power grids, ports, or telecommunications networks, it could complicate U.S. contingency planning and make coming to the defense of its allies more difficult.

Although BRI projects are diverse, they tend to share a number of common features:

- Chinese companies involved in BRI projects usually enjoy state backing and access to significant amounts of cheap credit, which allows them to take on projects that other companies could deem too risky or too costly.

- The Chinese state-owned commercial banks and policy banks that provide financing have far more resources to devote to infrastructure projects than most other lenders and a prior directive from Beijing to embrace BRI projects.

- Loan terms are rarely publicly disclosed, and because China has refused to join the Paris Club of major official creditors, Chinese banks are under no pressure to cap lending rates or share information.

- Once a BRI project is identified, the loans extended to host countries are generally made on close-to-commercial, rather than concessionary, terms and are not tied to economic or political reform, making them more accessible to states with existing debt or governance issues.

- Few governance metrics have been established for projects, and many are pursued without conducting financial viability or environmental- or social-impact assessments. Chinese companies generally push to begin projects quickly in an effort to reduce transaction costs.

- Chinese lenders often are willing to continue projects even when they encounter significant political and financial obstacles.

To be sure, Chinese banks and companies were active in foreign markets prior to BRI, so not all of the concerns over China's approach to foreign investment can be laid at the feet of BRI. What BRI did, however, was turbocharge these patterns. Chinese companies and banks looked to capitalize on Beijing's new policy pronouncement and garner political favor by quickly finding projects that could be placed under the BRI umbrella. Inevitably, this race led to Chinese banks backing projects that were not economically sustainable and to Chinese companies prioritizing speed over quality. BRI ushered in a frenzy of lending and construction that often led to a further erosion of standards. In addition, bad BRI projects are more enduring than Chinese investment that is not linked to the initiative: Chinese actors are motivated to continue BRI projects, even in the face of evidence that they are not sustainable, because this is Xi's signature initiative. Beijing has also ensconced the initiative into numerous multilateral organizations and pacts, giving BRI staying power and deeper reach than traditional Chinese foreign investments.

Many BRI countries appreciate the speed at which China can move from planning to construction, its willingness to build what host countries want rather than telling them what they should do, and the ease of dealing with a single group of builders, financiers, and government officials. Although the United States can contend that Chinese methods are unsustainable and come with many pitfalls, it would be a mistake to assume China is imposing its development model on BRI countries that do not want it.

Beijing's implementation of BRI has been uneven. BRI has brought infrastructure to countries sorely in need of such investment, relieving power shortages, easing economic bottlenecks, and allowing local products to get to the market quicker, thus improving people's livelihood. On the other hand, some large projects have stalled, others never got off the ground, and still others are being renegotiated because they are economically unviable. Many BRI projects are beset by corruption. Critics within numerous developing countries charge that Chinese firms do not hire enough local workers and therefore do not transfer enough knowledge or expertise, nor provide much economic benefit to the host country. In a case that has become most synonymous with the perils of BRI, Sri Lanka ceded control of a port for ninety-nine years to a Chinese company because it could not repay its debt on a BRI project.[26]

Unsurprisingly, many leaders of developing countries have grown more skeptical of BRI. Some U.S. analysts fear that BRI will saddle countries with debts they will never be able to repay, lead countries to become economically dependent on China, provide significant opportunities for the Chinese military to project power, and lay the foundation for a Sinocentric world order.[27]

Responding to mounting criticism of BRI, Xi has pledged to reorient the initiative to focus more on poverty alleviation and health care and to emphasize green development. He has highlighted the need for economic and fiscal sustainability of projects and pledged that BRI will follow international standards for project development.[28] As China has tried to adjust BRI and head off further criticism, the COVID-19 pandemic has greatly complicated its efforts, forcing many projects to a standstill and making recipient states, now in economic distress, more aware of their debt problems.

Implications for the United States

No matter how China adjusts BRI for a post-pandemic world, the initiative will continue to have important implications for the United States. In facilitating market entry in many countries for Chinese companies and lowering the costs of working with those Chinese companies, BRI often tilts the playing field toward Chinese firms. With support from state-owned banks, Chinese companies—many of which are also state owned—could displace U.S. exports and challenge U.S. companies in BRI countries. If countries are unable to pay back BRI loans and end up in a debt crisis, global macroeconomic stability could be undermined as well.

China's push to export its technologies to dozens of BRI countries also poses challenges. Most developing countries have significant needs for telecommunications infrastructure, data centers, and cloud services, which have grown even more urgent because of the COVID-19 pandemic and the shift to remote work. BRI allows China to meet these needs more cheaply and in a more coordinated way than the United States or its allies. By building next-generation digital networks across the world, China could gain access to vast amounts of data, which could help it build artificial intelligence (AI) technologies and which it could exploit to gain sensitive data from other countries and exfiltrate it back to China.[29] China's efforts to dominate next-generation digital networks could also lock other states into Chinese technological ecosystems incompatible with products made by non-Chinese firms. Such a development, though far down the road, could close off many markets in developing countries to non-Chinese firms.

BRI further increases the chances that China will successfully set technical standards governing industrial processes and telecommunications in many countries. Although China's attempt to craft technical standards predates BRI, the initiative has allowed Chinese companies to increase their market power, better enabling them to set standards that could be incompatible with those of non-Chinese firms. Depending on how they are used, Chinese surveillance technologies exported along BRI could make authoritarian regimes' repression more efficient. China's growing strength in producing and selling digital goods could permit it to export views on internet governance that are at odds with U.S. positions. Chinese companies' growing role in providing technology-driven financial services (fintech) risks locking millions of consumers in BRI countries into using apps developed by these Chinese companies for their banking needs, with an increasing number of transactions settled in yuan and a digital Chinese currency on the horizon.

China also has shown a willingness to use economic leverage for political advantage, and although this strategy predates BRI and is not limited to BRI countries, the initiative gives China greater leverage in more places. China could translate BRI's economic influence to economically punish countries that take positions on issues at odds with Chinese interests and employ economic inducements to convince countries to promote China's preferred positions. With such leverage over BRI countries, China could be better able to shape discourse on contentious issues related to China's domestic and foreign policies, including its persecution of the Uyghur minority, its crackdown on freedoms in Hong Kong, and its militarization of the South China Sea (SCS).

This leverage could be important in the security realm. China could use its increased investment in and influence over ports in BRI countries to project power into new regions and possibly to collect intelligence on the U.S. military, if the United States also uses these same ports and other facilities. In addition, in places where Chinese firms have built critical infrastructure, such as telecommunications networks and power plants, and in which Chinese firms retain operational control of this infrastructure, China could turn off a country's power grid or telecommunications network to force the recipient country to take actions preferred by China. Beijing could use this leverage to pressure a country to deny access to U.S. forces.

BRI projects will also make it harder to address global climate change. By exporting coal-fired power plants and building carbon-intensive infrastructure in other countries, China is not only generating huge carbon emissions but also locking countries into decades of carbon-intensive growth.

In prioritizing the distribution of medical supplies, personal protective equipment (PPE), and health technology to its BRI partners, China is using the COVID-19 pandemic to build its brand of charitable support, while using its position as the world's largest producer of medical goods, PPE, medicines, and active pharmaceutical ingredients (API) to deepen its commercial ties to BRI countries.

In many of these areas, China has used the size of its significantly protected domestic market, the financial power of its state-owned banks, and the political backing of the CCP to develop highly capable companies ready to build hard and digital infrastructure around the world under the auspices of BRI. China has also taken advantage of a vacuum the United States has created through a confluence of its own actions, including

- reductions in federal funding for research and development (R&D);

- an inability to field competitive alternatives in critical technologies, such as fifth-generation (5G) cellular networks and high-speed rail;

- a failure to craft modern trade rules and join multilateral trading blocs;

- the withdrawal from or decreased participation in multilateral organizations;

- a disengagement from standards-setting bodies; and

- a retreat from providing global public goods.

Unless the United States strengthens its nascent response to BRI, it should expect China to leverage its accomplishments and continue to employ opaque lending and contracting practices to enhance its presence and power in BRI countries.

FINDINGS

The Task Force finds that BRI presents significant risks for U.S. economic, political, climate change, security, and health interests. As it evaluated these implications, the Task Force also examined how the COVID-19 crisis, and the accompanying wave of economic distress, is reshaping BRI.

The Task Force has sought to avoid conflating BRI with all of Chinese foreign policy, but doing so is admittedly difficult given the initiative's broad, amorphous nature. Rather, the Task Force has attempted to evaluate the independent effects of China's push to export traditional and digital infrastructure via BRI in each of these areas and provide a comprehensive assessment of the capital, goods, services, technologies, people, and ideas moving under the BRI umbrella.

Economics

Despite potential gains for the United States, BRI poses significant risks to U.S. economic interests.

BRI's size and scope give it the potential to boost global gross domestic product (GDP) by as much as $7.1 trillion by 2040 and reduce global trade costs by up to 2.2 percent.[30] It promises to provide much-needed financing to developing countries, helping build the infrastructure necessary to erase blackouts, ease transportation bottlenecks, and make many economies more globally competitive. The United States, even if not formally part of BRI, would likely benefit in some ways if BRI builds infrastructure that accelerates global economic growth.

Were U.S. companies able to sell equipment and material required in the production, maintenance, or operation of the infrastructure built in BRI countries, those U.S. firms would stand to profit. To the extent that modern infrastructure lowers transportation and communications costs in BRI countries, U.S. producers trading with and operating out of those countries would also benefit. Global political stability usually accompanies sustained economic growth, and the United States would benefit from greater stability throughout the developing world.

The actual implementation of BRI, however, makes it likely that the costs will considerably outweigh the benefits for the United States. BRI has added to some participating countries' debt levels to an unsustainable extent. BRI projects are tied to Chinese contractors and conducted through a largely closed bidding process, excluding firms from the United States and many other countries. Because Chinese workers do most of the construction and then operate the newly built facilities, the transfer of know-how and training of local workers is limited.[31]

China's push to set technical standards through BRI and its banks' ability to provide subsidies to firms building BRI projects will likely tilt the playing field in some countries away from non-Chinese multinational corporations, as well as local firms. In many BRI countries, the United States will struggle to keep pace with China as Chinese firms rapidly gain market share and Chinese technical standards become the norm.

When these emerging debt crises in BRI countries materialize, they will undermine global economic growth and macroeconomic stability at a time when the COVID-19 pandemic has already led to the sharpest global economic contraction since the Great Depression. Debt crises also have the potential to increase the risk of a financial crisis.[32] Countries that go through a debt crisis will likely endure a long-lasting economic contraction, which would lower demand for U.S. exports.[33] A debt crisis that occurs amid a pandemic would be even more catastrophic, as the country would likely be forced to cut back on social services in order to meet debt obligations, which could hamper efforts to contain COVID-19 and deal with its aftermath. Finally, debt distress that results in countries leasing back major projects or collateralizing a high percentage of their loans means more countries could become economically dependent on China, which China could leverage to extract political concessions in ways that undermine U.S. interests.

> BRI creates unfair advantages for Chinese companies, leaving U.S. and other foreign companies unable to compete in a number of BRI countries.

Although Beijing consistently emphasizes that BRI projects are open to all bidders and that it would welcome partnerships with foreign companies on projects, Chinese companies still win the vast majority of BRI contracts. An examination of the contractors participating in Chinese-funded projects shows that 89 percent are Chinese companies, 7.6 percent are local companies (companies headquartered in the same country where the project was taking place), and 3.4 percent are foreign companies. Projects funded by MDBs, however, favor local contractors

(40.8 percent), with a rough split between Chinese (29 percent) and other foreign companies (30.2 percent).[34] China has used BRI to help propel its construction contractors into global leaders, holding the top five and seven out of the top ten spots in the ranking of global contractors in the world. No U.S. firms are even in the top twenty today.[35]

China has successfully used its development model to create industrial champions. The process often starts with a state-supported Chinese company importing technology (either legally or through coercion or sometimes theft) from foreign firms. These Chinese firms then adapt that technology while significantly increasing their output, production processes, and experience, selling into a domestic Chinese market often protected in some ways by tariffs or other regulatory barriers from import competition. The large Chinese domestic market allows these firms to grow into huge companies, often building sophisticated and well-honed production processes, which they then use in export markets, including in BRI countries. Aided by state-backed financing on favorable terms to the companies, these firms are then well positioned to win construction contracts and many other deals in export markets, particularly in developing countries. A significant portion of the Chinese goods sold represent excess production that is looking for a home, so Chinese companies often sell at prices far below what market-based companies can offer.

China's push to export high-speed and standard-gauge rail along BRI provides an example of this development model in action. After energy, BRI's most ambitious, expensive, and closest-to-completion undertaking is to build railroad lines transporting goods and people from China across Central Asia to Russia and Europe, along with additional lines running from southwestern China throughout Southeast Asia and railroads in Africa and Latin America. To develop its railroad system from one in which trains moved at an average speed of nineteen miles per hour in 1993 to one in which, just fifteen years later, sleek trains moved at nearly 220 miles per hour, China began by leveraging its vast domestic market to import foreign technology and adapting the technology at home.[36] Beijing has built more miles of high-speed rail domestically than the rest of the world combined.

As China became saturated with high-speed rail lines, it sought to export its excess capacity and identified BRI as the perfect conduit. As with other sectors, railroad construction allows Beijing to export excess capacity, particularly steel, and to secure more reliable sources for needed inputs. China is providing subsidies to BRI countries to facilitate the purchase of Chinese rail, which is displacing rail built by multinationals from other countries, in particular Canada, France, Germany, Japan, and South Korea.[37] Although it is unclear whether the economics justify the cost of constructing these rail lines through Central Asia, Southeast Asia, and other regions, they will help reorient economies toward China.

China is growing its financial technology companies, which use BRI to gain privileged access to millions of consumers while potentially giving Beijing major surveillance opportunities.

The World Bank estimated in 2017 that nearly two billion adults lack access to a bank account or mobile money provider.[38] Such unbanked individuals rely on cash, which can be unsafe and hard to manage, and find it difficult to navigate financial emergencies without access to more sophisticated financial services.

Chinese financial technology companies—defined as those employing technology-enabled innovation in financial services—have been quick to address this unmet need in a number of BRI countries, particularly in Southeast Asia and Africa. Although Chinese private companies are driving outward expansion of Chinese fintech, they often use the BRI or Digital Silk Road label to gain domestic political support for their overseas commercial expansion and leverage the market access provided by BRI projects.[39]

China's fintech companies have grown significantly in recent years.[40] China's largest fintech company, Ant Group, has rapidly expanded its reach overseas, investing in banks, insurance companies, and payment systems providers.[41] Ant's mobile payment app, Alipay, is estimated to have more than 1.3 billion users, 900 million in China and the rest concentrated in BRI countries, which represents nearly four times as many users as the largest U.S. mobile payments company, PayPal.[42] Close on Ant's heels is Tencent, which has been pushing its WeChat Pay into a number of BRI markets, particularly Indonesia, Malaysia, Russia, and Thailand.[43]

Because fintech companies depend on vast amounts of data and AI to optimize their offerings, China is well positioned to dominate this sector. Alipay and WeChat Pay, for example, generate a significant amount of data on spending, cash flows, and credit evaluations through their control of more than 90 percent of the huge mobile payments market in China.[44] Because China already has the largest e-commerce market in the world, data generated from its digital marketplace provides a strong backbone for fintech expansion into other countries; encouragement and subsidies from the government, particularly for the development of data storage infrastructure, have facilitated fast growth for Chinese fintech companies (although the recent shelving of Ant Group's initial public offering signals that the Chinese government will likely seek to rein in some activities of Chinese fintech firms).[45] These fintech firms can use a vast amount of data to provide smarter and more customized services to both individuals and small- and medium-sized enterprises (SMEs) in foreign countries, including those along BRI.[46]

Beijing is also focusing on blockchain ledgering. Chinese leaders believe that blockchain technology will be the foundational infrastructure for future technological innovation, and in 2020 Beijing launched the Blockchain Service Network (BSN).[47] BSN is designed to leverage blockchain technology to offer software developers a cheaper alternative to current server storage space offerings.[48] A number of major blockchain projects have joined BSN, integrating their own chains with it, thereby enabling developers to create applications on the larger, less expensive BSN.[49] Such integration also allows Beijing to bring this "international plumbing," including the network infrastructure in Australia, Brazil, France, Japan, South Africa, and the United States, under its influence.[50] As China's BSN white paper noted, "Once the BSN is deployed globally, it will become the only global infrastructure network autonomously innovated by Chinese entities and for which network access is Chinese-controlled."[51]

Many BRI countries welcome Chinese fintech companies, which could bring more people and small businesses into modern banking and offer affordable lending, insurance, and payment services. Some countries, however, have resisted China's fintech platforms because they cut out countries' central and local banks, can make it harder to account for financial flows, and risk hardwiring their banking system to the Chinese economy.[52] Both Indonesia and Nepal, for example, have barred individuals and businesses from processing Alipay and WeChat Pay payments for these reasons.[53] Some analysts have expressed concern that Chinese firms' dominance over BSN, which could provide Beijing influence over blockchain networks outside China, presents security risks comparable to those raised regarding Chinese firms' control over 5G networks.[54] If illicit actors were to use applications built on BSN, the United States' ability to take cryptocurrency-related enforcement actions or to prosecute those violating U.S. law related to certain cybercrimes could depend on cooperation from China for the digital data evidence needed to make a law enforcement case. Similar concerns arise over China's fast-moving plans for a digital renminbi, called the Digital Currency/Electronic Payment (DCEP), to replace its physical currency. DCEP's design gives China's central bank real-time financial surveillance of all users' transactions, potentially bolstering the government's control over private behavior and adding to the reach of its "digital authoritarianism."[55]

The COVID-19 pandemic is accelerating the trend of slowed lending and increasing debt distress.

Prior to the pandemic, China's BRI lending had already shown signs of slowing, a result of slackening demand, efforts by Beijing to raise lending standards, and attempts by Chinese banks to deleverage.[56]

Even before the pandemic, the probability that BRI countries would be unable to repay their loans was increasing, with the World Bank estimating nearly one-third of BRI countries to be at high risk of debt distress because of underlying macroeconomic weaknesses.[57] By the end of 2019, an estimated $20 billion of BRI projects had been delayed, with another $64 billion put on hold, and $12.6 billion canceled.[58] BRI also had run into a series of problems as countries such as Malaysia and Myanmar renegotiated BRI projects to lighten their debt burdens, convinced they were unsustainable and structured to primarily benefit China.[59] Other capital-intensive BRI projects in Kyrgyzstan, Nepal, Serbia, Sierra Leone, Tanzania, and Thailand were scaled back, canceled, or stalled.[60]

The economic fallout of COVID-19 has accelerated these trends. BRI lending continues to slow—China's Ministry of Foreign Affairs announced one-fifth of BRI projects had been "seriously affected" by COVID-19—and is likely to remain at a more moderate pace.[61] Even if China wanted to continue to fund BRI at its pre–COVID-19 pace, it could not, as lockdown restrictions impede Chinese firms' abilities to send workers and materials to construction sites abroad.[62] Demand for Chinese loans has fallen, because BRI countries cannot be sure they can generate the economic growth necessary to pay them off. With less margin for error in the face of a global economic recession, BRI has likely entered a new phase of smaller, more rigorous lending to projects that have greater chances of success. BRI's smaller scale means that the benefits and risks of BRI are likely to be reduced moving forward.

> COVID-19–induced crises are exposing the debt sustainability problems brought on by BRI.

Debt struggles in many BRI countries predate the initiative, and BRI is one of many factors contributing to countries' debt distress. At the same time, BRI has exacerbated debt distress, and China's approach to lending and debt restructurings often compounds these issues.

China's BRI lending differs from development finance provided by traditional lenders, and the global economic contraction brought on by COVID-19 has exposed the shortcomings of China's lending approach:

- BRI is predominantly financed by debt, with most projects backed by two state-run policy banks, the China Development Bank (CDB) and the Export-Import Bank of China (China EXIM), and some state-owned commercial banks.[63] CDB, the world's largest provider of development finance, has committed $250 billion to fund BRI projects.[64]

- China's central bank provides massive capital injections to China's policy banks, which also enjoy low borrowing costs. These advantages allow China's policy banks to subsidize operations linked to BRI and be less demanding than other multinational banks in their lending criteria.[65]

- In contrast to loans from traditional providers of development finance, China's loans are generally not concessional, and CDB and China EXIM expect to make a return on their investments.[66] The loans also lack policy conditionality; they contain few or no expectations of host country economic or political reforms.[67]

For many BRI countries, especially authoritarian regimes, this is an attractive package, especially compared with other lenders, who insist on reforms tied to loans.

BRI projects also often omit many of the feasibility and debt sustainability studies conducted by other multinational lenders and move forward rapidly in an effort to reduce project transaction costs.[68] The COVID-19 pandemic has revealed the danger in relying on debt issued at close-to-market rates, because the economic shock has made it significantly harder for many countries to repay their BRI loans. This prioritization of speed, ostensibly driven by a desire to increase efficiency, increases the risk that a project will not be able to pay for itself.[69]

Although not setting explicit debt traps, China's lending practices contribute to debt crises along BRI.

China has often been accused of using BRI to set "debt traps"—intentional Chinese efforts to load countries with unsustainable debt that will allow Beijing to seize assets or induce political concessions when debts go unpaid—but there has yet to be a case in which China has taken control of other countries' infrastructure.[70] The notion is largely based on one case—the $1.1 billion Hambantota Port project on Sri Lanka's southern coast. Sri Lanka's president, motivated by a desire to develop his home district, initiated this project with China, and most of Beijing's involvement in the port predated BRI. The ninety-nine-year leasing of the port to a Chinese SOE in 2017 was the result of numerous idiosyncratic factors, including Sri Lanka's preexisting crippling debt (largely to commercial creditors), balance-of-payments problems, a natural disaster, civil war, and the government's decision to privatize state assets, allowing China to bid on the port.[71]

Although BRI countries often do encounter trouble financing projects and seek to renegotiate loan terms, renegotiations often cut in favor of the host country, with Chinese companies accepting losses, calling into question whether a debt-trap strategy would even benefit China.[72] In addition, China incurs reputational costs when BRI projects fail. Hambantota is now invoked to demonstrate the perils that come with accepting Chinese financing. The notion of debt traps also robs BRI countries of agency: host governments determine the nature of BRI projects in their countries and have to approve projects and take on the

Figure 3. RENEGOTIATIONS OF CHINESE DEBT ARE MULTIPLYING, AND COVID-19 IS FORCING MORE

Source: Rhodium Group.

related loans. BRI countries pursue projects that they believe are in their interests; China cannot simply foist unwanted projects on countries.[73] Yet, although actual asset seizure may not be the norm, the risk is clear that countries unable to repay their debts to China could become clients of China, deferring to it on political or strategic issues.

Nonetheless, economic stress brought on by COVID-19 could make some BRI projects unsustainable and lead to accusations of debt-trap lending, regardless of China's intentions. The initiative suffers from a self-selection process whereby many countries opt for BRI projects because they have poor macroeconomic fundamentals and nowhere else to turn for financing. The COVID-19 pandemic has derailed many BRI countries' already shaky economies, quickening the reckoning with BRI-related debt. Given the long time horizon necessary for large infrastructure projects to generate the growth necessary to pay for themselves, COVID-19 increased debt distress at a time when most BRI projects are not producing any revenue for the host countries. Debt renegotiations have now multiplied, with more on the horizon (see figure 3).

> Better deployment of international financial institution (IFI) resources, along with debt relief, is required to meet the needs of vulnerable countries during the COVID-19 pandemic.

The International Monetary Fund (IMF) estimates that the COVID-19 pandemic caused the world economy to contract by 3.5 percent in 2020—the most severe global economic cataclysm since the Great Depression.[74] The poorest countries have been among the hardest hit, as they lack policy tools to cushion the blow and have experienced capital flight and remittance loss.[75] In February 2020, the IMF found that more than half of the world's low-income countries were in, or at high risk of, debt distress.[76] As of June 2020, a major credit rating agency had downgraded to negative its outlook on at least fifteen BRI countries.[77] Foreign exchange pressures have also led to a near doubling in debt servicing costs.[78] The pandemic has raised the specter of a significant emerging market debt crisis.

Major lenders have tried to respond. In March 2020, the IMF made an open-ended pledge to deploy as much of its $1 trillion of lending capacity as needed to shore up member economies.[79] So far, the IMF has provided over $100 billion in financial assistance to 85 of its 189 members and has extended over $280 billion in total lending commitments.[80] In addition, MDBs have approved $57 billion of support for needy countries.[81] Nearly all of these funds have gone to developing countries. BRI countries—Bangladesh, Egypt, Indonesia, the Maldives, Nigeria, Pakistan, and the Philippines, among others—are among the leading recipients of this international assistance.

Still, a sizable gap remains between the needs of BRI countries and the amount of assistance currently being offered by the IFIs and MDBs. The IMF estimates that emerging markets need at least $2.5 trillion in financing to weather COVID-19–related economic shocks, far greater than what has been pledged.[82] New financing from the IFIs cannot meet all of these needs. BRI countries, including Djibouti, Laos, Maldives, Pakistan, and Zambia, among others, have flooded Beijing with requests for renegotiations of loan terms and debt forgiveness.[83] Kyrgyzstan announced that it had worked out a settlement with China EXIM, its largest single creditor, to reschedule $1.7 billion of debt repayments.[84] CDB has extended its credit line to Sri Lanka by $700 million, lowered the interest rate on loans, and delayed repayment, and Sri Lanka has requested a new $500 million loan from Beijing.[85] Nonetheless, numerous debt renegotiations loom on the horizon.

China's efforts to address emerging debt crises along the Belt and Road have been insufficient.

Before the pandemic, China had begun to respond to criticism of its lending practices by

- signing on to the Group of Twenty (G20) Operational Guidelines for Sustainable Financing;

- partnering with the IMF to set up a training center in Beijing to help countries improve their ability to assess debt sustainability;

- inking a memorandum of understanding (MOU) with eight MDBs, establishing a Multilateral Cooperation Center for Development Finance;

- endorsing the G20 Principles for Quality Infrastructure Investment; and

- publishing a debt sustainability framework for BRI that it asserted was similar to the standards used by the IMF and World Bank.[86]

To date, China has not taken enough action on these pledges. China's policies are critical to any global debt relief efforts, as it is by far the largest sovereign creditor to the world's seventy-three poorest countries.[87] In response to the pandemic, China has notionally signed on to IMF, World Bank, and G20 debt suspension initiatives.[88] Beijing, however, initially insisted that its policy banks, which issue the bulk of BRI loans, are exempt from the Debt Service Suspension Initiative and similar debt relief pledges.[89] Only after sustained international pressure did China relent and agree to enter into renegotiations to restructure China EXIM loans, which account for approximately 30

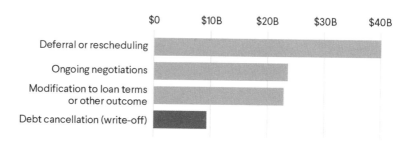

Figure 4. CHINA RARELY CANCELS DEBT, PROLONGING DEBT DISTRESS

Renegotiated debt by outcome, January 2001 to November 2020

Source: Rhodium Group.

percent of total BRI loans.[90] Still, indications are that China continues to insist that CDB loans are ineligible for the Debt Service Suspension Initiative.[91] China's stance underscores its understanding of these projects as commercial ventures rather than pure development activities and risks forcing BRI participants to choose between meeting debt-service requirements to China or funding local economic recovery and critical medical services at a moment of historic crisis.

China is likely to resist canceling many debts related to BRI projects even in the face of this global crisis and will instead push to extend the grace period of loans, increase the maturity of the loans, reschedule payments, and extend lines of credit (see figure 4).[92] For example, China agreed to give Kyrgyzstan a deferral on $35 million in debt repayments due in 2020 but added a 2 percent interest rate to the amount.[93] China rarely cancels debt, the exception being the relatively small percentage of its lending that is foreign aid given on an interest-free basis. China is likely to push for private bilateral negotiations with each of the BRI countries and make decisions on a case-by-case basis.

China will continue to use ad hoc BRI arrangements to gain access to BRI country markets.

Xi Jinping has emphasized BRI's goal of "advanc[ing] the building of free trade areas and promot[ing] liberalization and facilitation of trade and investment."[94] China's thirteenth Five Year Plan committed to a swift process of fulfilling Xi's wish, stating, "We will speed up efforts to implement the free trade area strategy, gradually establishing a network of high-standard free trade areas. We will actively engage in negotiations with countries and regions along the routes of the Belt and Road Initiative on the building of free trade areas."[95]

Until the Regional Comprehensive Economic Partnership (RCEP) was signed on November 15, 2020, however, little progress had been made in negotiating such free trade agreements. Started by the ten members of the Association of Southeast Asian Nations (ASEAN), RCEP adds Australia, China, Japan, New Zealand, and South Korea, resulting in an agreement connecting nearly 30 percent of the world's people and output. All RCEP members except Australia and Japan are also BRI countries, thereby creating baseline rules governing trade, investment, intellectual property protection, government procurement, and competition policy for this subset of BRI countries.

Many of the rules in RCEP do not extend much past the basic World Trade Organization (WTO) trading rules. The agreement's provisions on e-commerce, digital trade, competition, and government procurement, however, as well as the important rules of origin that permit inputs from any RCEP country to be counted together when determining whether a good qualifies for RCEP preferences, are significant.[96] Because many of the tariffs on goods traded among RCEP members are already low or will not change as a result of the agreement, RCEP could have limited immediate economic effect.[97] RCEP can, however, be expected to incentivize supply chains to operate within the region and to enhance the gains from BRI's strengthened transport, energy, and telecommunications links among RCEP members.[98] RCEP also signals a greater willingness among these Asian countries to work together without the United States. The agreement is likely to promote further integration of these economies and solidify China's position as the center of Asian trade and investment.

RCEP notwithstanding, China has few trade or investment agreements with its other BRI partners. Outside of RCEP, the lack of deep, transparent agreements establishing reciprocal market access between China and its BRI partners has given China more flexibility, as its ad hoc BRI arrangements are more opaque and contain fewer basic requirements. One-off bilateral deals also give little indication about whether any increased access to BRI markets, including to the Chinese market, will be available to others or limited to preferential access for firms pursuing a BRI project. Moreover, the ad hoc, secretive nature of most BRI contracts makes it difficult for countries to take collective action in responding to China should they believe the terms of the contracts are unfair.

What is clear is that China's trade with BRI countries has been growing more rapidly than its trade with non-BRI countries. In 2019, China's total trade with BRI partners was $1.34 trillion, 7.4 percent higher than its aggregate growth in trade.[99] China's exports to BRI countries also far exceeded its imports, in part because BRI countries have imported a significant amount of construction equipment and building materials from China. For the United States, the absence of transparent agreements establishing basic market access, contract, and procurement rules leaves U.S. companies uncertain of what their rights could be should they wish to participate in BRI projects.

> Despite the global economic slowdown, BRI countries will continue to seek Chinese loans and Beijing will continue to fund BRI projects.

China's own debt burden and its need to devote resources to boosting economic growth at home have raised questions about its ability to continue funding BRI, particularly if forced to choose between investing more in its own economy or in BRI countries.[100] BRI lending, however, remains a small portion of Chinese banks' overall investment portfolios. Chinese policy banks enjoy strong political support and have ample room to continue to lend to BRI countries. At the peak of BRI, China was estimated to have lent $50 to 60 billion annually, a fraction of the $2.6 trillion in annual Chinese bank lending.[101] BRI's two main funders, CDB and China EXIM, had committed only 2.9 percent and 3.1 percent of their assets, respectively, to BRI as of the end of 2018.[102] In addition, given that other multinational lenders outside of China are retrenching at a moment of upheaval, China can lend at a smaller scale than it did prior to the pandemic and still make a significant impact on recipient states and potentially generate political goodwill as well.

BRI will endure as countries continue to request that Beijing fund additional projects, despite the global economic cataclysm and their rising debt burdens, and as China maintains the capacity to lend. For example, despite the fact that the signature China-Pakistan Economic Corridor (CPEC)—an initiative that is explored in more detail below— was already behind schedule and over budget, in July 2020 the two countries announced $11 billion of new rail and hydropower projects in the corridor.[103] That same month, China also announced a twenty-five-year, $400 billion slate of investments in Iran, for which it will receive a regular and heavily discounted supply of Iranian oil in exchange.[104]

Although China will continue to build traditional infrastructure in BRI countries, it will likely shift its emphasis toward less costly yet influential projects through the Digital (DSR) and Health Silk Roads (HSR):[105]

- After the COVID-19 outbreak, senior Chinese government officials have emphasized that digital projects could help BRI countries' economic recovery.[106] In December 2020, Chinese Foreign Minister Wang Yi signaled Beijing would make this shift, declaring the "Digital Silk Road is a priority area for BRI cooperation in the next stage."[107]

- Moreover, the pandemic itself is likely to generate demand for DSR projects in BRI countries as economic activity continues to move online.[108]

- Finally, faced with the increasing prospect that they could be excluded from the U.S. market and those of U.S. allies in Europe and Asia, Chinese telecommunications and internet companies want to boost their market share in other regions and could redouble their DSR efforts in Africa, Central Asia, and South and Southeast Asia.[109]

Spotlight: The China-Pakistan Economic Corridor—Hard Reality Greets BRI's Signature Initiative

During an April 2015 visit to Islamabad, Xi Jinping and Pakistani Prime Minister Nawaz Sharif unveiled the $46 billion CPEC, BRI's flagship initiative and its most ambitious undertaking in any single country. Beijing hoped to leverage its close partnership with Islamabad to build new transportation and power infrastructure across the country, succeeding where the United States had failed and providing a model that other BRI countries could follow.[110] Left unspoken were China's hopes that CPEC would open up a direct route between China and the Indian Ocean, that a prosperous Pakistan would no longer be a hotbed of extremism, in turn stabilizing Xinjiang and securing China's periphery, and that a stronger Pakistan would advantage China over its strategic competitor, India, and by extension the United States.

CPEC quickly ballooned to $62 billion in pledges—one-fifth of Pakistan's GDP—covering dozens of envisioned high-profile projects. The derelict port of Gwadar, located on the Arabian Sea at the mouth of the Strait of Hormuz, emerged as CPEC's jewel. China planned to transform it into a modern port, build supporting infrastructure, and establish a free trade zone next to the port. Most CPEC funds, however, have gone to building new coal-fired power plants to help Pakistan overcome its crippling power shortages. Other prominent projects included a $7 billion upgrade to the railway from Peshawar to Karachi, two hydroelectric power plants in the disputed Kashmir region, a metro system in Lahore, the establishment of multiple special economic zones (SEZs), and Huawei fiber-optic cables running from China to Pakistan (see figure 5).

Pakistani Prime Minister Sharif called CPEC a "game changer," and it did improve Pakistan's infrastructure, reduce its blackouts, create tens of thousands of jobs, and boost economic growth.[111] At the same time, CPEC was plagued by stalled projects, reports of corruption, and terrorist attacks. A Pakistani government committee concluded that Chinese contractors were overcharging Islamabad by $3 billion on two CPEC power plants, and reports emerged that Chinese investors were guaranteed large annual returns on their investments.[112] Almost no commercial shipping calls at Gwadar, and the Lahore metro appears to be economically unviable.[113] Although Pakistan formed a fifteen-thousand-person security force to protect CPEC construction, it was not enough to prevent a string of terrorist attacks.[114] Pakistanis began to criticize CPEC, arguing that China benefited more from the initiative than Pakistan, and in response CPEC was effectively put on hold and then rebooted in a slimmed-down package.

Although Pakistan's economic woes preceded BRI, CPEC sparked a further rise in the country's debt. The IMF warned that CPEC was contributing to a widening current-account deficit, as the country imported billions of dollars of materials for the projects.[115] Pakistan soon experienced a balance-of-payments crisis and turned to the IMF for a three-year, $6.3 billion bailout.[116] Pakistan began undertaking the painful reforms necessary to get its economy back on track, but because of COVID-19 its economy contracted in 2020.[117] Pakistan is now looking to delay debt repayment to China for a decade and drastically cut the interest rate on loans from Chinese banks.

Ultimately, CPEC is unlikely to ever fulfill the grand vision laid out in 2015.[118] Going forward, CPEC instead will comprise smaller projects with less potential economic impact. CPEC has been a humbling experience for China; if it could not pull off transformative development in a country with which it enjoys strong ties and shares a border, then it will have to scale back its ambitions in other BRI countries.

Even with CPEC's shortcomings, the initiative has the potential to bolster China in its growing geostrategic rivalry with India. With control of the Gwadar port in Pakistan and the Hambantota port in Sri Lanka, as well as construction of the Payra port in Bangladesh, China's navy has the potential to gain access on all sides of India.[119] China has been pressing Pakistan to strengthen its control over contested areas of Kashmir because Beijing wants to avoid the appearance of CPEC projects being built in disputed territory.[120] As a result, negotiation over the Kashmir issue will become more remote, and China could use its economic leverage over Pakistan to encourage it to take a more aggressive position vis-à-vis India in an attempt to weaken New Delhi.

CPEC has implications for U.S. interests. The United States does not necessarily need to worry about new roads, railways, or even ports

Figure 5. THE CHINA-PAKISTAN ECONOMIC CORRIDOR IS BRI'S SIGNATURE UNDERTAKING

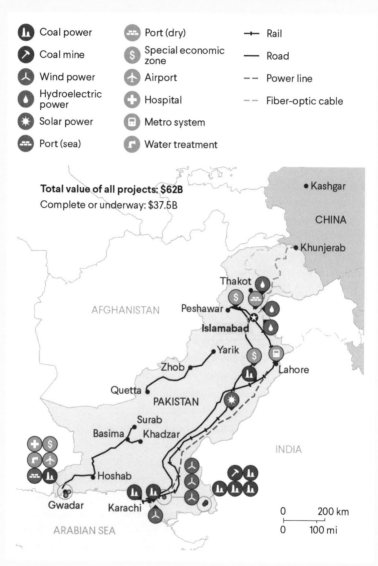

Names and boundary representations are approximate and not necessarily authoritative.

Sources: Government of Pakistan; CFR research.

being built in Pakistan. The United States should welcome them if they are economically viable and contribute to Pakistan's economic growth and political stability. At the same time, with a retired Pakistani general now overseeing CPEC's implementation and China working primarily through the Pakistani army to smooth out any political or economic issues and silence critics, the initiative has strengthened the Pakistani military's role in society, further eroding the country's democracy.[121] Building telecommunications infrastructure and fiber-optic cables in Pakistan also has the potential to enable Pakistan to crack down on civil liberties and spread Chinese internet governance norms. China has also ensured that a prominent Muslim country on its border will not speak out as it continues to persecute its Uyghur minority.[122] In exchange, China has used its seat on the UN Security Council to shield Pakistan-based terrorist groups from terror designations and international sanctions.[123] Finally, because Pakistan has access to another source of largely unconditional aid, the U.S. ability to marshal Pakistan's support on regional issues and counterterrorism is diminished.

Politics

China's investments along BRI have increased its soft power, but such gains are fragile and have shown signs of reversal.

BRI projects have a strong signaling value, furthering a narrative in host countries that their future prosperity is inextricably tied to strong relations with Beijing. Even the European Union (EU), with seventeen of its twenty-seven member states signing on to BRI, entered into the EU-China Comprehensive Agreement on Investment (CAI) in December 2020, despite an admonition from the incoming Joe Biden administration to wait and join forces with the United States on a common approach to China.[124] Although the CAI gives European companies invested in China some market access assurance, for China it represents a major geopolitical victory, furthering the story of a strong country with deep economic ties in Europe standing tall on the world stage.[125] Heads of state converge on Beijing for Belt and Road forums, where they hear from Xi Jinping and sign deals for infrastructure projects along with joint communiques that thank China for hosting such events.[126] At the Second Belt and Road Forum, UN Secretary-General Antonio Guterres lauded BRI's "immense potential," praised it for having "sustainable development as the overarching objective," and pledged the "United Nations system stands ready to travel this road with you."[127] BRI can thus be seen as an integral element of a broader strategy to bolster China's geopolitical influence and international standing.[128]

In large part because of BRI, many believe China is a more significant economic actor than the United States, even though U.S. private-sector investment usually outstrips Chinese investment. Although U.S. firms invest globally, they are not seen as appendages of the state, and often, publics do not even know these are U.S. companies. Those U.S. firms participating in BRI projects often do so as subcontractors or background service providers such that U.S. logos may never appear at a construction site. By contrast, the presence of Chinese firms is much more visible. Thus, although the stock of U.S. direct investment in Southeast Asian countries outweighs investment by Chinese companies, a survey of Southeast Asians revealed that 79 percent of respondents believed China had the most economic influence in Southeast Asia, while only 8 percent believed the United States was the preeminent economic power in the region.[129] Fifty-two percent believed China was also the most influential political and strategic actor, compared with 27 percent for the United States, and 47 percent expressed little or no confidence in the United States as a strategic partner.[130]

The same pattern holds in Africa, where the stock of U.S. direct investment on the continent remains higher than Chinese investment, but publics perceive China to be the most influential economic actor.[131] A survey of people in thirty-six African countries found that they believe China exerts more external influence in their country than the United States, trailing only their former colonial power. The most important factor contributing to this assessment was China's investment in infrastructure on the continent, driven by BRI.[132]

Although BRI has the potential to strengthen China's hard and soft power, missteps with some projects, corruption scandals, increasing awareness of debt burdens, resentment over the substantial inflow of Chinese labor displacing local workers, and the loss of local autonomy over projects have combined to limit BRI's contribution to the growth of China's power. Public protests in BRI countries have become increasingly common. In Sri Lanka and Cambodia, for example, citizens have protested being displaced for BRI projects and not receiving promised compensation.[133] The same survey of Southeast Asians revealed that 64 percent have little or no confidence in BRI, and 72 percent of those who view China as the most influential economic power are worried about its growing economic influence.[134]

> BRI abets corruption and democratic backsliding in host countries.

Major infrastructure projects provide ample opportunities for corruption, and BRI's practices magnify these opportunities. Opaque lending terms and contracts and closed bidding processes typify BRI projects. This secrecy and lack of accountability enables corrupt political elites to award contracts to their allies and divert funds toward their supporters. BRI does not include an anticorruption mechanism for monitoring projects, nor have Chinese companies cracked down on local partners for misusing funds. Chinese banks and companies often carry out BRI with domestic political actors they are most comfortable with, skirting democratic institutions and tying the fate of projects to the continued success of individual politicians and political parties.

BRI investment has often shored up authoritarian regimes when they are most vulnerable, providing financing they desperately need after countries cut off aid and financial ties in response to concerns about human rights abuses. As a result, the United States and like-minded countries lose leverage that they would have otherwise enjoyed to pressure these countries to improve their governance.

Malaysia's experience highlights how BRI provides an opening for corruption and rent-seeking behavior. China embraced Malaysian Prime Minister Najib Razak and greenlit multiple megaprojects that were not economically feasible but could bolster Najib's political standing. Najib diverted funds to greasing his patronage network and maintaining electoral support. When sovereign wealth fund 1Malaysia

Development Berhad (1MDB), which Najib used as his personal slush fund, could not repay $13 billion it had borrowed, he approached China for a bailout. The sides agreed to $34 billion in new BRI projects despite conceding they lacked "strong project financials," with the goal of inflating their price tag so that Chinese SOEs could assume 1MDB's debts and use excess funds to pay down other 1MDB debts.[135] Najib was voted out of office in large part because of these scandals, put on trial, and convicted on all counts. Jho Low, a major figure in the 1MDB scandal, is wanted by multiple countries but is reportedly living in China under the government's protection.[136]

China's willingness to support corrupt politicians, work around democratic institutions, and bail out countries that are committing human rights abuses is evident across BRI:

- In Kyrgyzstan, in one of BRI's first projects, China EXIM lent $386 million to rebuild the power plant that provided nearly all of the capital's heat and electricity. China's embassy made clear that its preferred contractor had to be chosen for the project, and eventually $111 million was siphoned off, with the Chinese contractor purchasing fire extinguishers for $1,600 and pliers for $320.[137] Following an investigation, dozens of officials, including a former Kyrgyz prime minister, were charged with corruption.

- Myanmar, shunned by the United States for committing genocide against its Rohingya minority, has embraced BRI for its financing needs, inking over three dozen deals with China.[138]

- Sri Lanka, largely avoided by investors because of human rights abuses during its civil war, turned to China for funding an array of projects. China worked closely with President Mahinda Rajapaksa, backing economically unfeasible megaprojects in his home district to boost his party's electoral prospects. The Chinese SOE building the port at Hambantota funneled funds away from the project and directly to Rajapaksa's election campaign.[139]

- In Pakistan, China invested heavily in its relationship with Prime Minister Nawaz Sharif and his Pakistan Muslim League-N party (see Pakistan Spotlight). It worked primarily with Sharif and his brother, Shabhaz Sharif, and many BRI projects disproportionately rewarded Sharif's Punjab political base. In response to current Prime Minister Imran Khan's publicly opposing much of BRI during his election campaign, China decided to go around Pakistan's embattled democratic institutions and instead began working directly with the military on BRI.[140]

BRI has increased the supply of surveillance technology to autocratic and struggling democratic regimes.

Chinese firms, led by Huawei, are the world's leading suppliers of AI surveillance technology used for public security.[141] These "safe city" programs, as Huawei terms them, encompass everything from facial recognition technology to video surveillance systems. Because DSR projects tend to package technology in bundles, recipient states are more likely to purchase potentially worrisome technologies as part of a broader information, communications, and technology (ICT) buildout.[142] The same technology that monitors traffic flows and assigns parking tickets is also used for the digital surveillance of citizens, for example. Chinese firms are hardly the only surveillance technology providers: many companies headquartered in liberal democracies are both offering similar products or enabling Chinese companies to field their technologies.[143] However, Chinese firms are the primary suppliers in twenty-four countries; of these, fourteen are BRI participants. Although 44.1 percent of BRI countries have acquired AI surveillance technology from Chinese companies, only 26.4 percent of non-BRI countries have done the same.[144] Nonliberal regimes are also much more likely to sign safe city agreements with Huawei.[145]

DSR makes it easier for countries to acquire surveillance technology, providing authoritarian states with greater capabilities to entrench themselves and monitor their populations. Huawei employees aided Uganda's president, who has ruled the country for more than three decades, in spying on his political opponents, intercepting their encrypted communications, and tracking their movements. In Zambia, another BRI country, Huawei employees accessed the phones and social media pages of opposition figures at the behest of the Zambian government, leading to concerns of democratic backsliding.[146] In both instances, the Chinese equipment that underpins such surveillance was provided as part of DSR.[147]

Through DSR, Chinese companies have also undertaken safe city projects in Kenya and Uganda and provided mass surveillance facial recognition technology to Zimbabwe, making political repression more effective.[148] Beijing provides government-to-government training programs for DSR states, which could help them improve intelligence collection against and monitoring of their own citizens.[149] China could also help countries better control their internet services and monitor their citizens' social media activity.

Surveillance technology exports through DSR will not turn a democratic country into an authoritarian one, but they could be used to cement authoritarian control where it already exists or abet a mixed regime's backsliding. Furthermore, the relative growth of China's smart cities offerings and dearth of alternatives means that the Chinese supply will likely only increase over time in relative terms.[150]

Spotlight: BRI in Kenya—Providing Needed Infrastructure, but at a Cost

The trajectory of BRI in Kenya belies fears of a neocolonial debt trap, but the initiative's lack of transparency has exacerbated Kenya's endemic corruption. Although BRI has built critical infrastructure in the country, including Kenya's most expensive infrastructure project since independence, Chinese missteps and failure to build support among Kenyan institutions and within civil society have raised Kenyan concerns about the benefits of BRI.

China has long sought to invest in and build economic linkages with Africa, and Kenya reciprocated interest under its Look East policy.[151] Chinese policymakers viewed Kenya as a prime opportunity because of its strategic location as a "maritime pivot point" offering access to East and Central Africa and its ability to serve as a conduit for raw materials, including Sudanese and Ugandan oil.[152] From Kenya's perspective, Chinese investment in national megaprojects could help Kenya replace its dilapidated infrastructure and accelerate its economic development.[153] Although Kenya enjoys access to international capital markets, it had been unable to finance desired infrastructure projects before China stepped in.

Some Kenyan leaders have embraced BRI, with President Uhuru Kenyatta attending both of China's BRI Forums. Three major BRI projects have taken shape in the country:

- expanding Mombasa Port, the region's largest port

- building a deep-sea port and related infrastructure at Lamu

- laying a standard-gauge railway (SGR) across the country (see figure 6)[154]

In addition, Huawei also built Africa's first safe city system in Nairobi, deploying cameras and surveillance systems in an attempt to reduce crime, and rolled out a similar system in Mombasa.[155] Prior to BRI, China had been a relatively minor lender to Kenya, providing

$2.2 billion to the country in the thirteen years before BRI was announced. Since 2014, however, China has extended almost $7 billion in loans to Kenya, most of which has gone toward the railway, considered a flagship BRI project in Africa.[156]

Despite mounting controversy, Kenyan and Chinese leaders have lauded the railway, which opened in 2017.[157] It represents a major improvement over the country's outdated rail lines, cutting travel time between Nairobi and Mombasa, Kenya's two largest cities, in half and providing expanded rail shipping capacity. But its $3.8 billion cost raises concerns that the project cannot pay for itself.[158] The line loses nearly $10 million a month, its debt service will be burdensome, and Mombasa Port serves as collateral for the railway loans.[159] Although China is unlikely to seize the port if Kenya cannot service its rail loans, that possibility gives Beijing leverage over Kenyan political decisions. In addition, the railway contract was awarded without a competitive tender, with funding contingent on using Chinese contractors to build and operate the railway.[160] The project has now become mired in disputes, legal issues, parliamentary inquiries, and corruption investigations, and Kenya's effort to extend the railway to the Ugandan border and beyond has faltered.[161]

BRI efforts in Lamu, a UN Educational, Scientific and Cultural Organization (UNESCO) World Heritage Site, have also sparked backlash over pollution, environmental damage, and population displacement concerns.[162] A greenfield port and supporting infrastructure at Lamu is intended to anchor the Lamu Port South Sudan-Ethiopia Transport Corridor, which also includes highways, oil pipelines, a railway, airports, and resort cities.[163] Work has begun at the new deep-water port, where China is building the first three of thirty-two expected berths under a $484 million contract.[164] However, dredging for the port has destroyed local marine life and habitats, prompting the High Court of Kenya to order significant compensation for local fishermen.[165]

The lack of transparency surrounding BRI projects has encouraged corruption and exacerbated ethnic polarization. Kenya regularly falls among the bottom third of nations in corruption perception rankings, and BRI project opacity creates an environment in which corruption can flourish.[166] Kenya's Ethics and Anti-Corruption Commission

Figure 6. BRI PROJECTS REPRESENT KENYA'S LARGEST INFRASTRUCTURE INVESTMENT SINCE INDEPENDENCE

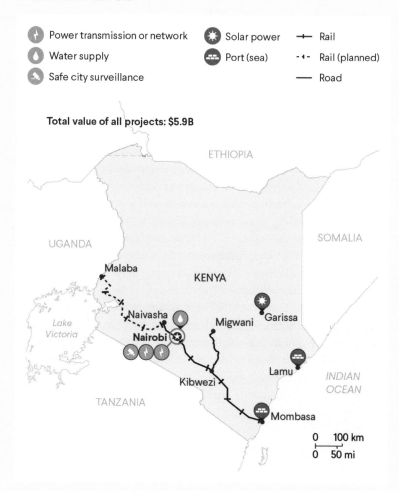

Names and boundary representations are approximate and not necessarily authoritative.

Source: CFR research.

suspended land compensation around the rail line, for example, because of allegations of graft.[167] Meanwhile, the hands-off nature of Chinese firms building BRI projects enables local Kenyan partners to award jobs and supply contracts along tribal and ethnic lines, exacerbating ethnic polarization in the country.[168]

Even though Kenya has managed to both participate in BRI and preserve its other relationships better than some host countries, it faces a difficult path ahead. The economic viability of Kenya's BRI projects has deteriorated.[169] The World Bank assesses that the combination of BRI debt and the economic shock of COVID-19 has left Kenya at high risk of debt distress.[170] China is Kenya's biggest lender; interest payments to Chinese entities represented 87 percent of cash used to service Kenya's debt in 2019.[171] Kenya will likely need to renegotiate its debt with China in the near future.[172]

Kenya is a long-standing economic and security partner of the United States and a significant regional economy.[173] The United States continues to invest in its relationship with Kenya, and it has formally elevated the bilateral relationship to a strategic partnership, established an annual strategic dialogue, and launched negotiations for a bilateral free trade agreement. Many U.S. companies have their regional headquarters in Nairobi, because Kenya remains East Africa's most important commercial and financial hub, but China's presence complicates U.S. efforts to foster a close partnership with Kenya.

> BRI provides China with economic leverage that it employs
> for geopolitical advantage.

China has long sought to translate its economic influence over countries into political leverage, attempting to gain veto power over other nations' strategic decisions or punish them for choices Beijing opposes. China pressured Cambodia to block ASEAN resolutions critical of Chinese practices in the South China Sea, retaliated against South Korea for its decision to employ the Terminal High Altitude Area Defense (THAAD) missile defense system, impounded Filipino imports to show its displeasure over the government's SCS claims, placed restrictions on Norwegian salmon to punish the country after the Nobel Peace Prize was awarded to a Chinese dissident, and successfully pressured Greece and Hungary to block the EU from criticizing China at the UN Human Rights Council.[174] More recently, when Australia called for an investigation into the origins of COVID-19, Beijing levied tariffs on a dozen Australian products and ordered traders to stop buying various Australian commodities.[175]

By linking economies to China and making countries depend more on Chinese finance, BRI provides Beijing with additional geopolitical leverage. China's goal is clear: to make countries reliant on access to the Chinese market and Chinese finance for economic growth while ensuring China becomes more self-sufficient for its own needs. In speeches to international audiences, Xi Jinping has publicly underscored China's commitment to economic liberalization, but to members of the CCP, he has stressed the need to "tighten the dependence of the international industrial chain on China."[176]

Examples of BRI countries accommodating China's strategic interests while amassing increased Chinese investment are numerous. Nepal, a BRI country that counts China as its largest investor, in recent years has reinforced its border at China's request to curtail the arrival of Tibetan refugees and repatriated Tibetans to China, where they face severe repression.[177] In the midst of renegotiating major BRI projects and arranging a bailout for its crisis-ridden sovereign wealth fund 1MDB, Malaysia appealed to China by noting it had publicly voiced support for Beijing's SCS territorial claims during a regional summit.[178] As China has come under global criticism for the mass internment of its Uyghur Muslim minority, Pakistan, which has the world's second-largest Muslim population and is the largest recipient of BRI funds, has refrained from criticizing China. When asked about this during a 2019 conversation at the Council on Foreign Relations (CFR), Imran Khan stated, "We don't make public statements, because that's how China is … I would not publicly talk about it."[179]

> China could use BRI to promote Chinese legal standards while exporting its model of authoritarian development.

If a less transparent, poorly governed approach crystallizes into a model used along BRI corridors, opaque and risky projects could become the norm, along with the political and legal advantage these bestow on Beijing. Most BRI projects take shape through informal, partnership-based, or relational approaches, rather than the more rules-based approach used by the United States in the form of bilateral investment Treaties (BITs), free trade agreements, or the multilateral rules of the WTO. As a result, many of the norms being created by individual BRI agreements are not transparent and are often negotiated in countries that lack strong legal norms for complicated transactions spanning all aspects of commercial, financial, and investment law.

The Supreme People's Court of China has published model cases focusing on common BRI issues, clarifying some commercial rules and calling for the uniform application of laws, but these model cases serve only as guidance for disputes brought in lower Chinese courts and so are unlikely to create transparent norms. Moreover, by engaging in opaque, case-by-case contracting, China makes it difficult for countries to compare notes to understand the relative value of projects or act collectively to push back on unfair terms.

More recently, China established two international courts to handle BRI disputes. Given how common disputes are in complex construction ventures, these Chinese courts or the more well-established forums for international arbitration in Hong Kong, London, New York, and Singapore are likely to face increased caseloads. Legal analysts worry that BRI disputants could come under pressure to settle in the new Chinese courts.[180] Although China claims these courts will avoid the current combination of local courts and international arbitration that is "complicated, time-consuming, and costly," another motivation could be to develop a venue that applies Chinese law in proceedings conducted in Mandarin as a way to protect Chinese companies.[181]

Promoting these new courts could also further a broader goal of effectively exporting China's legal norms as parties to BRI contracts come under pressure to hire Chinese-trained lawyers to handle the contracting and dispute resolution process, in the process weakening international law and the rights of BRI host countries.[182]

China could also use the training of foreign officials under the auspices of BRI as a tool to spread its views on economic development and governance. People-to-people exchanges and training foreign political figures, officials, and scholars is a pillar of BRI.[183] Xi also added an "educational Silk Road" to BRI, and China has set up Silk Road scholarships.[184] As part of BRI, the Chinese Academy of Sciences (CAS) has more than 1,300 graduate students studying and conducting research in China and trains two hundred PhD students each year.[185] CAS has also opened up nine research and training centers in BRI countries in Africa and Asia and co-funds research projects in many more of its BRI partners. As part of BRI, China has created the Alliance of International Science Organizations (ANSO), which brings together scientific research organizations from around the globe, including UNESCO.[186]

Whereas China is leveraging BRI to form linkages with up-and-coming scholars, the United States has chosen to reduce the number of outreach educational programs it offers and make it more difficult for foreign students to study in the United States. In the future, scholars and researchers could have fewer ties to the United States and more experience collaborating with Chinese academics. The United States also faces a future in which many officials in foreign governments will have been educated in and influenced by China, with few U.S.-educated officials in those ranks.

Spotlight: BRI in Italy—Creating Divisions in Europe

Italy's signing of an official BRI MOU during Xi Jinping's trip to Rome in 2019 angered other EU members as well as the United States. Italy's move raised fears among many in Europe that China would use its Italian connection to drive a wedge between the EU member states and weaken the union's foundation.[187]

So far, it appears Italy's decision to join BRI is largely symbolic. By signing on to BRI despite warnings from EU officials and the United States, Italy was attempting to leverage its political weight as the first Group of Seven (G7) country to endorse BRI, in hopes of beating out other BRI partners for Chinese attention and investments. After visiting Italy, however, Xi Jinping moved on to France, where he announced significantly more investment, even though Paris did not sign on to BRI. This contrast reveals that a country does not need to formally join BRI to receive Chinese investment, nor does endorsing BRI guarantee Chinese investment will increase.[188]

Italy's government was anxious to lift the Italian economy out of its third recession in a decade, and BRI seemed to offer a lifeline. At the time, many Italians felt abandoned by Europe over the immigration and economic crises that preceded the COVID-19 pandemic and were more than willing to turn to China to fulfill Italy's needs for increased investments in infrastructure and telecommunications. When Italy, experiencing the most severe outbreak of COVID-19 in the early days of the pandemic, pleaded for face masks and PPE for its medical workers, China responded by providing masks, ventilators, and three hundred intensive-care doctors. China's actions prompted a mild threat from Italy's foreign minister aimed at Europe: "We will remember those who were close to us in this difficult period."[189]

The impetus for connecting Italy to BRI is also a historic one, as Italy served as a major terminus along the ancient Silk Road and both sides celebrate Marco Polo as an ambassador connecting the two nations.[190] The cultural connections remain, as Italy is home to the largest Chinese population in Europe,. and the two countries share deep connections to the production of fabrics, leather goods, and more.

Figure 7. BRI CONSTRUCTION AND FUNDING HAVE STRENGTHENED CHINA-EUROPE RAILWAY CONNECTIONS

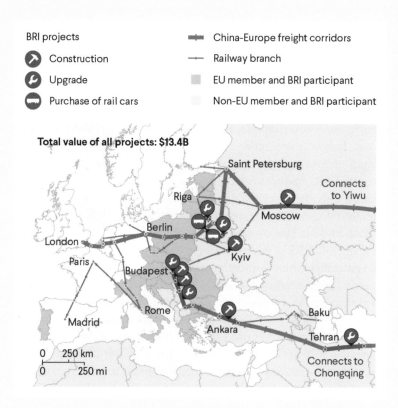

Source: CFR research.

How much BRI will meet Italy's economic needs remains to be seen. Since the MOU, Italy and China have signed nineteen institutional arrangements, covering everything from double taxation to recognition of certain sanitary requirements for pork exports and cultural property and heritage sites, as well as ten small commercial agreements. The stated goals are much bigger than actions to date, with deals in energy, finance, agriculture, gas, and engineering services mentioned, along with investments by China's Communications and Construction Company in the ports of Trieste and Genoa.[191] In addition, the China-Europe rail route has a terminus in the northern Italian town of Mortara, permitting direct rail shipments between Italy and China and ensuring Italy's inclusion in the major BRI thrust into railway services, dubbed an express lane to Europe by Chinese Premier Li Keqiang. Since Li's 2014 announcement, new construction has tied preexisting railroad tracks into one pulsing, transcontinental network, stretching from Yiwu on China's Pacific coast to London and Helsinki, Finland. Faster than container ships and cheaper than cargo planes, travel by these routes has fueled an explosion in Chinese freight, with a record 12,400 shipments traveling from China to Europe in 2020 (see figure 7).[192]

Italy's decision to publicly embrace BRI pushed a significant intra-European reckoning over BRI. Rumors of Italy's BRI moves likely contributed to the European Commission's and the European External Action Service's swift release of a strategic action paper bluntly referring to China as "an economic competitor in the pursuit of technological leadership and a systemic rival promoting alternative models of governance."[193] The EU then adopted a common plan for risk assessments related to national security to issue nonbinding opinions on foreign investments in critical sectors of any EU country.[194] Still, Italy's endorsement of BRI has not prevented it from taking a tougher stance on Huawei, as Rome vetoed a deal between Huawei and Italian telecommunications provider Fastweb in 2020 that would have used Huawei as the sole supplier for its 5G core network.[195] Italy's move nonetheless prompted efforts to maintain an EU-wide approach to BRI.

Climate Change and
Environmental Degradation

BRI is likely to remain a major source of growing global carbon emissions and lock countries in to high-carbon infrastructure.

Most BRI projects to date have focused on the transportation and energy sectors because of China's excess capacity in these areas and demand from BRI countries.[196] Through BRI, China is offering both the technology and the financing to build power plants, in most cases proceeding with coal-fired power plants despite Chinese expertise in renewable energy. BRI countries frequently request coal-fired power for several reasons. Many government officials are more familiar with coal-fired power, and their domestic energy policies often explicitly call for it. Coal is also perceived to be cheaper, more reliable (particularly for large baseload power), and easier for older grid systems to absorb.[197]

China is willing to respond to this demand. BRI countries know that if they want coal-fired power, China is the leading, and increasingly the only, source for financing coal-fired power plants.[198] Under the Barack Obama administration, the United States restricted its government financing for new coal-fired plants overseas and worked to block similar funding by the World Bank, which formally tightened its policy in 2018 to severely restrict such financing.[199] The Asian Development Bank has not funded any coal-fired power plants since 2013, and the China-led Asian Infrastructure Investment Bank (AIIB) also placed some limits on coal-fired power financing. In 2020, Japan and Korea, the second- and third-largest investors in coal-fired power after China, both announced they would no longer finance overseas coal power.[200] In light of the cutbacks by the MDBs and other major investors, Chinese banks are the world's largest source of financing for coal-fired power plants.[201]

As a result, more than 60 percent of China's BRI-specific energy financing from CDB and China EXIM has gone toward nonrenewable energy resources.[202] Between 2014 and 2017, 91 percent of energy-sector syndicated loans from six major Chinese banks to BRI countries were in fossil fuels, with 40 percent of BRI lending for the power sector in 2018 going to coal projects (see figure 8).[203] Although China has become the world's leading producer and user of renewable energy, it is now involved in as many as 240 coal-fired power plant projects across twenty-five BRI countries, including more than a dozen in Bangladesh alone.[204] In EU enlargement countries Bosnia and Herzegovina and Serbia, China has built and is building coal-fired power plants that do not meet EU environmental standards, including one that is Europe's largest sulphur dioxide polluter. At least six additional MOUs between Chinese companies and southeast European governments stipulate building more coal-fired plants.[205]

Building these coal-fired plants has allowed China to find work for its laborers and transfer its oldest and dirtiest plants out of the country after the enactment of regulations and taxes on carbon emissions within China. Cambodia was the recipient of one such coal-fired power plant that was completely disassembled in China and then reassembled by Chinese workers in Cambodia.[206] For the past nine years, China's coal consumption has been greater than the rest of the world combined, but it still mines more coal than it needs, and BRI helps its SOEs establish new markets for Chinese coal abroad.[207] At least thirteen BRI countries experienced double-digit growth in CO_2 emissions in the initiative's

Figure 8. MOST OF CHINA'S ENERGY PROJECT FINANCING IN BRI COUNTRIES GOES TOWARD NONRENEWABLES

Energy projects financed by Chinese banks in BRI countries since the initiative's launch in 2013

● Coal   ● Other nonrenewable (biomass, gas/LNG, oil)
● Renewable (wind, solar, hydropower)

$10B
$50M

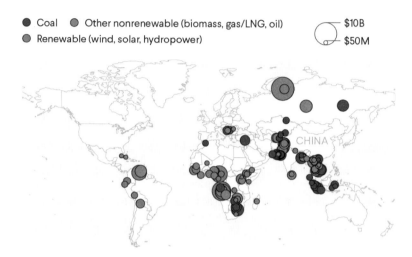

Sources: Boston University; Johns Hopkins University's School of Advanced International Studies' China Africa Research Initiative; Stimson Center; CFR research.

earliest years, and these increases beset countries that are already among the most affected by climate change, including Bangladesh, Myanmar, Pakistan, and Vietnam.[208]

A continued failure to reorient BRI toward low-carbon options could lead to "carbon lock-in" in recipient countries' economies because of the long-lived nature of the projects. Because each new coal-fired power plant is likely to last thirty-five years or more, such production commits many BRI countries to continued dependency on carbon-intensive power production. Although the COVID-19 pandemic could force China to shift away from expensive energy projects, demand from developing countries is likely to remain strong as they seek interim strategies to rehabilitate their economies and promote growth.[209] The fossil fuel energy projects undertaken through BRI will make it harder and more expensive for countries to scale down production in the long term, fixing the emissions rates of host countries at dangerously high levels and making it more difficult to respond to climate change.[210]

BRI projects threaten biodiversity, forests, and water resources.

Preserving critical habitats and national protected areas is not a major variable affecting China's overseas lending decisions. One database that tracks loans extended by CDB and China EXIM found they have funded 261 projects located in critical habitats and 124 projects in nationally protected areas.[211] BRI exhibits this pattern of largely setting environmental considerations aside. Many BRI projects, particularly those in the transportation and energy sectors, traverse environmentally sensitive areas, including protected areas and important spaces for biodiversity and birdlife.[212]

A report commissioned by Cambodia's government concluded that a hydropower dam being built as part of BRI was located at the "worst possible place," would do "devastating" harm to fisheries, and had the potential to "literally kill" the Mekong River.[213] Because many of the BRI corridors pass through steep terrain that is vulnerable to erosion, soil degradation, and sedimentation, the direct effects on the land, ecosystems, and wildlife could be elevated.[214] Poorly constructed roads can cause increased sedimentation in rivers and raise the risk of flooding. In Myanmar, for example, twenty-five million people live downslope from two proposed BRI road projects at risk of flooding.[215]

Further, the high-speed rail that makes up much of BRI's rail program requires straight lines that cannot be quickly routed around natural barriers, rivers, or lakes.[216] Virtually all railroad and road construction results in some degree of habitat destruction, particularly if traversing a tropical forest. Roads and railroads also fragment the habitat of wildlife, potentially creating barriers to migration. Moreover, the increased connectivity and the creation of new travel routes significantly raise the risk of the introduction of invasive species that could wreak havoc on native ecosystems.[217]

The development that accompanies BRI projects is likely to set in motion further unintended consequences as people move and markets shift in response to changes in transportation costs, which can open previously unoccupied land to settlements, resulting in habitat loss and deforestation. Although sound environmental assessments and a commitment to modifications to address environmental harm could mitigate many of these harmful outcomes, BRI projects often proceed without environmental impact assessments or mitigation efforts.

China's dam projects along the Mekong River showcase the need for careful environmental assessments and coordination with its BRI partners. All five countries in the Lower Mekong region—Cambodia, Laos, Myanmar, Thailand, and Vietnam—have officially endorsed BRI, which includes an effort to improve connectivity between China's southern provinces and Southeast Asia by building bridges and dams along the Mekong River and its tributaries.[218]

For its part, China operates eleven of the world's largest dams on the river, allowing Beijing to store more than forty-seven billion cubic meters of water and generate 21,310 megawatts of electricity.[219] But those dams, and China's refusal to join the regional group designed to coordinate policies affecting the river's health, the Mekong River Commission, have raised fears that Beijing could one day coercively restrict or shut off the water flow. And in 2019, China held back so much water from the river that it led to devastating shortages in Cambodia, Laos, and Thailand.[220] The downstream countries experienced a shortfall so severe that it resulted in the lowest water levels ever recorded in Thailand and left some riverbeds dried up entirely.[221]

The devastation caused by the low water levels in the spring of 2020 led some critics to contend that even the release of water has become political and something for which China seeks gratitude, with others claiming that China is guarding against climate change–induced loss of water by building massive water storage capacity behind its Mekong dams.[222] Even Cambodia's Prime Minister Hun Sen, one of China's staunchest allies and a major BRI supporter, was so concerned by the lack of water in the Mekong that Cambodia postponed until 2030 any further action on its two planned dams.[223]

China's pivot to an "open, green, and clean" BRI has few tangible results.

In response to international pressure, Beijing has endeavored to rebrand BRI as a green initiative, but its efforts have been underwhelming. This is largely because China's new guidelines are purely voluntary and it has been unwilling to impose environmental standards on host nations, requiring instead that BRI projects meet local environmental standards, no matter how low those standards are.[224] The most effective greening initiatives to date could be the adoption of Green Investment Principles (GIP) for Belt and Road Development and the establishment of a BRI International Green Development Coalition (BRIGC).[225]

The GIP are the result of a joint exercise by the City of London Corporation's Green Finance Initiative and China's Green Finance Committee, drafted by representatives from the World Economic Forum, UN Principles for Responsible Investment, Belt and Road Bankers Roundtable, and the Paulson Institute.[226] They aim to create common standards for what constitutes a green project and to embed principles of sustainable development across all types of financing and all phases of a BRI project, along with requiring financial institutions to conduct environmental impact assessments for their BRI investments. If adhered to, the GIP would do much to stop the problem of "greenwashing" that plagues investments from around the world, by prohibiting using in-name-only "green bonds" to finance the replacement of small, inefficient coal plants with larger, more efficient but fundamentally high-carbon facilities and other only marginally green projects.

The fundamental problem with China's efforts to make BRI more environmentally sustainable is that these principles remain voluntary, and though a number of Chinese and European banks have signed on, few developing country institutions have joined the initiative. Yet green finance remains an area where China has shown a stronger commitment and ability to influence the direction of BRI investments.

The BRIGC also shows significant promise in that it creates an international network of environmental ministries, nongovernmental organizations (NGOs), researchers, and international agencies working to promote the UN's sustainable development and environment goals along BRI.[227] The UN Environment Program and the Chinese Ministry of Ecology and the Environment run the coalition, which includes participation from environment ministries in twenty-six BRI countries and 120 organizations, including the World Wildlife Fund, Client Earth, and the World Resources Institute. Work is underway for two-year and five-year plans, for draft guidelines for all BRI projects, and for the launch of pilot projects in the near term.[228] It is not clear, however, whether the coalition can overcome strong differences among its members or address the fundamental problem that the only required compliance for BRI projects is with a host country's environmental regulations.

Security

BRI port projects have significant strategic implications for the United States but are unlikely to become a network of Chinese military bases anytime soon.

Within the First Island Chain in the western Pacific, China's maritime ambitions include asserting its sovereignty over disputed features and territories and establishing regional preeminence; beyond the region, its aims are currently more modest and include access to ports, influence in other countries, and protecting its overseas interests, including access to critical supplies.[229] As the world's largest energy importer, China worries that in the event of a conflict with the United States, U.S. forces could blockade the straits of Malacca, cutting off the vast majority of China's energy supply. Beijing's push to secure sea lines of communication by building and gaining access to ports along the Maritime Silk Road can be understood as an attempt in part to address its "Malacca Dilemma."[230] A functioning port at Gwadar, and a pipeline connecting it to China, would theoretically allow China to bypass the straits of Malacca and help relieve this dilemma.

Beijing worries that it lacks the access arrangements necessary to protect its substantial overseas interests, with its national defense white paper noting "deficiencies in overseas operations and support."[231] To remedy this shortcoming, Chinese military strategists have argued the country should acquire "overseas strategic strongpoints" in the Pacific and Indian Oceans, and BRI's path includes these strongpoints.[232] China has no formal military alliances and currently has only one small overseas military base in Djibouti, used primarily to support counterpiracy and peacekeeping operations.[233] China is also reported to be building two new naval piers in Cambodia as part of a broader agreement giving China exclusive rights to a Cambodian naval station.[234]

China does not appear to be seeking a U.S.-style network of overseas bases and access agreements, nor does it yet have in place the operational concepts and organization to sustain large overseas military operations. Instead, the People's Liberation Army (PLA) could rely on access to a variety of commercial port facilities to support its operations and logistics overseas.[235] Chinese firms own, partially own, or operate at least ninety-three ports across the globe. Firms with close ties to the CCP own and operate many of these ports, which are concentrated near maritime chokepoints and critical sea lines of communication.[236] BRI is a tool to expand this influence. Under the auspices of BRI, Chinese banks have financed numerous ports around the world, while Chinese firms have retained ownership stakes in these ports.

By financing, constructing, and operating this vast network of overseas ports, China has gained varying degrees of control over major maritime commercial facilities, and Beijing recognizes the value of these facilities. According to a former Sri Lankan foreign secretary, for example, China made clear during negotiations concerning the Hambantota port that intelligence sharing would be a part of the deal.[237] Chinese military strategists acknowledge, however, numerous hurdles to using commercial facilities to sustain major military operations.[238] In some cases, if Beijing sought to project military power outside East Asia, it would need to recast existing ports to accommodate major warships and related maintenance and logistic activity.

In other instances, the PLA Navy (PLAN) would have few obstacles to overcome. Although Gwadar is not a PLA base and the PLAN has yet to make a port call at the facility, the Pakistan Navy operates Chinese-built ships out of the port, and thus it would not be difficult for the PLAN to use the same facilities and parts to sustain operations. Gwadar also has the ability to host the PLAN's largest vessels, and the port's lack of commercial activity and isolation make it a more desirable place from which to conduct military operations.[239] Accordingly, U.S. planners should remain attuned to the possibility that China could pursue a network of overseas bases, including at Gwadar, which offers a compelling logistics hub for the PLAN. But such a shift is unlikely to emerge in the near future, and should it occur, the United States would have significant warning time in which to respond. Until China secures true base access, its ability to use commercial ports in wartime is limited.[240]

Nevertheless, China's port control could have major strategic implications for host nations and for the United States. If the host is a U.S. treaty ally, its self-defense or wider regional contingencies could rely on the United States' ability to flow logistics in crisis or conflict. If that port is owned or operated by a Chinese entity with close ties to the government, Beijing could apply pressure, preventing or delaying the host country's reception of military logistics and supplies necessary for defense.

For example, COSCO, a Chinese SOE formerly controlled by China's Ministry of Transport, holds a majority stake in the port authority at Piraeus, Greece, and operates the entire port. A decision to close the port to U.S. forces could impair U.S. and North Atlantic Treaty Organization (NATO) operations against Russia. A similar risk is present in Haifa, Israel, where a Chinese company is poised to operate the port for the next twenty-five years. Such an outcome could have consequences for operations throughout the Eastern Mediterranean and Levant. Even without China's being able to use commercial ports as bases, Beijing could still deny the U.S. military the ability to use them. Such actions would substantially affect prospective U.S. operations in Asia, Europe, and the Middle East.

The COVID-19 pandemic is unlikely to change Beijing's maritime ambitions. In the short term, China's shipbuilding industry took a hit as a result of quarantines and stay-at-home orders, affecting completion deadlines.[241] PLA recruitment was temporarily halted, exacerbating a shortage of naval aviation pilots.[242] These delays have compounded ongoing limitations within the PLAN, including a lack of basic logistic and sustainment capabilities necessary for blue water operations.[243]

Despite these setbacks, China's strategic interest in port access abroad is likely to remain high. Locally, BRI port projects could be less likely to be canceled than other transportation projects, as they are often established through subnational authorities where local sentiments could be more eager to see the project to completion.[244] Acute debt crises could lead BRI port hosts to lease back port stakes or assets to China as they search for relief, which would increase China's levers of control over these vital nodes.

> China's port projects also have significant nonmilitary implications.

Less analyzed and understood are the nonmilitary advantages China could reap from its port projects. Companies closely tied to the Chinese government finance, construct, and operate overseas ports as part of BRI. Port financing could allow Chinese companies to win political advantages, reward supporters, or access resources in host countries. Port construction presents companies with intelligence collection possibilities, whereas operating the ports presents much greater intelligence-gathering opportunities with less chance of detection. Operating ports also could allow China to manipulate trade flows as a form of financial sanctions or to deny foreign actors' access to ports.[245]

China's port projects also give Beijing the opportunity to build commercial relationships with the host country and extend political goodwill:

- In some cases, China could gain an advantageous strategic position: better access to sea lines of communication; the prospective opportunity to improve its power position relative to a rival; or proximity to chokepoints that could help guarantee its energy security and freedom of action in crisis or conflict.

- It could gain the ability to control foreign access to ports, put dual-use facilities toward military purposes, and access commercial or financial data that is politically, economically, or militarily useful.

Figure 9. CHINA'S INVESTMENTS IN PORTS AND UNDERSEA CABLES HELP EXPAND ITS INFLUENCE

Ports in which a Chinese company has some ownership and undersea internet cables built by Huawei Marine

● Whole port owned by a Chinese firm — Completed cable
● Port terminal with majority ownership ⋯ Planned cable
● Port terminal with minority ownership ▨ BRI participant

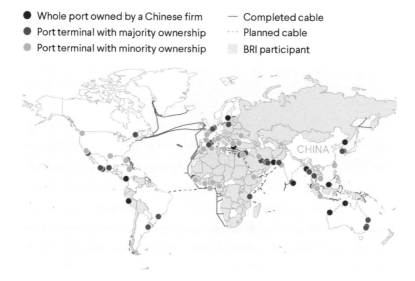

Sources: U.S. Naval War College's China Maritime Studies Institute; *Wall Street Journal*; Telegeography.

- Finally, it could acquire particular intelligence benefits if a port lies on a Chinese or foreign-built undersea cable terminal or near a U.S. military facility (see figure 9).[246]

The potential implications of Chinese ports for U.S. interests vary considerably depending on the form and extent of Chinese stakes in the ports, political circumstances of the host country, proximity to U.S. military facilities, and other factors (see figure 10). The United States should assume that a major port project will give China greater political and economic leverage with the host country. This risk would be even greater if the country is already indebted to China and more politically consequential if that country is a U.S. ally. In cases where a Chinese firm owns and operates the entire port (rather than just a single terminal) and has close ties to the Chinese government, and the host country is economically dependent on China, the United States could be especially likely to have its own military access denied in a period of heightened tensions.

The United States should also assume that China could eventually utilize a port facility for dual-use or military purposes, to sustain military operations of its own. This would, in turn, limit U.S. military freedom of action in the surrounding area. China could use ports to collect commercial data, while in other cases it could reap military intelligence benefits. Opportunities for consequential intelligence collection are higher at ports that serve as terminuses for undersea cable communications systems, and are likely to be especially high at port facilities operated by China that serve as terminals for Chinese-built undersea cable systems.

China's supply of energy technologies and its push for global energy interconnection give it potential control over vital infrastructure in BRI countries.

Xi Jinping is pursuing a vision of interconnectivity for power plants, transmission, and grid infrastructure, describing BRI's energy projects as increasing "mutual trust in politics and creat[ing] a new pattern of energy security featuring co-cooperation, mutual benefit and win-win results."[247] China's Global Energy Interconnection Development and Cooperation Organization (GEIDCO), an international organization made up of energy and construction companies, equipment manufacturers, financial institutions, research universities, and NGOs, in conjunction with the State Grid Corporation of China (SGCC), estimates that Beijing's total investment in power sources and grids in BRI countries will reach $27 trillion by 2050.[248]

With the help of Chinese financing, SGCC has already built grids that connect China to Laos, Mongolia, Myanmar, and Russia while investing in grid operations in Brazil, Italy, the Philippines, and Portugal.[249] China has built a combination of coal-fired, renewable (largely wind and hydropower), and nuclear power plants throughout Southeast Asia and Africa, in addition to energy facilities in Europe and Latin America, with estimates that nearly two-thirds of Chinese spending on completed BRI projects went into the energy sector.[250]

Figure 10. A STRATEGIC ASSESSMENT OF PORTS DEMONSTRATES THE RANGE OF BENEFITS TO CHINA

Port	Economic/ political	Strategic location	Operational control	Dual use/ military	Intelligence
Port of Zeebrugge Belgium	Medium	Low	Low	Medium	Low
Paranagua Port Brazil	Medium	Low	High	Medium-Low	Low
Doraleh Port Djibouti	High	High	High	High	High
Port of Piraeus Greece	Medium	Medium	High	Medium	Medium
Port of Haifa Israel	Medium	Medium	Medium	Medium	Medium-High
Lamu Port Kenya	Medium	Medium	Low	Medium-Low	Medium
Port of Mombasa Kenya	Medium	Medium	Low	Medium	Medium-High
Kyaukpyu Port Myanmar	Medium	High	High	Medium	Low
Gwadar Port Pakistan	Medium	High	High	High	High

Note: Belgium, Brazil, and Israel are not formal members of BRI but are included in this assessment to demonstrate the reach and strategic potential of China's investments in ports.

To see the full table of strategic assessments, including Chinese stakes in the ports, consequences for the United States, and reasoning behind the assessments, visit www.cfr.org/BeltAndRoad.

Source: CFR research.

Beijing's plan is to use the size and strength of SGCC, now the third-largest company in the world, to build out and then connect power grids, with a network of transmission and distribution grids connecting large energy bases under a smart, comprehensive platform that allocates energy and resources throughout the network.[251]

In recognition of the fact that connecting power grids across international boundaries requires some form of supranational governance, in 2016 China's SGCC set up GEIDCO to promote global energy interconnection. The UN Framework Convention on Climate Change embraced GEIDCO as an NGO partner, with officials from the UN and World Bank noting its potential to address problems of power shortages, poverty, and climate change. As a recent report noted, however, "The line is thin between GEIDCO's mission to 'serve the sustainable development of humanity' and its role in laying the ground work for huge SGCC contracts and Chinese-led infrastructure build."[252]

Although the construction of modern renewable power plants, coupled with the development of smart power grids, holds great promise for more efficient, sustainable energy markets, China's emergence as the leader in certain power technologies raises security concerns. The power grid interconnections rely on supervisory control and data acquisition systems running on communications and technology networks built by SGCC and other state-owned entities, giving China intelligence-gathering opportunities and the potential ability to manipulate or deny power to other countries. SGCC's Chairman Liu Zhenya referred to global energy interconnectivity as "the ICBM of the power industry."[253]

Because power grids constitute critical infrastructure, they are common targets for cyberattacks. Countries' abilities to fend off such attacks could rest in China's hands rather than their own if their power sources or power grids are partially or fully owned by Chinese SOEs. Chinese companies could also take outright control of power grids in BRI countries. Heavily indebted Laos, struggling to make debt payments to China in the face of the COVID-19 pandemic, ceded majority control of its electric grid to a Chinese state-owned company, and others could follow.[254] All of this makes it more likely that China, through its ability to control power grids in BRI countries, will gain the ability to push its policy preferences on these countries.

BRI enables Chinese technology companies to penetrate and dominate markets.

Announced in 2015, the Digital Silk Road is a more focused undertaking than BRI writ large. A handful of China's national champions—Huawei, ZTE, China Mobile, China Telecom, Alibaba,

Tencent, Baidu, and JD, as well as a few others—are encouraged to build out digital infrastructure in BRI countries, with less overlap and a clearer division of labor.[255] China's Ministry of Industry and Information Technology has provided clear direction to these companies, identifying six core areas for DSR: 5G technology, smart cities, utilization of the Beidou satellite system, communication infrastructure, network connectivity, and telecommunications services.[256]

Under DSR, indigenous Chinese ICT firms receive state backing that gives them three sets of advantages:

- First, companies such as Huawei, Hikvision, and ZTE gain preferential government treatment through policy support and major lines of credit through CDB, China EXIM, and state-owned commercial banks.[257] This in turn allows them to sell their products 30 to 40 percent more cheaply than non-Chinese competitors.[258]

- Second, Beijing also extends credit to specific DSR projects and countries to allow them to make major purchases from Chinese companies. For example, China EXIM financed 85 percent of the China-Pakistan Fiber-Optic Project and loaned to Nigeria the full cost of a Huawei-built 5G network.[259]

- Third, policy backing and pricing advantages allow Chinese companies to receive preferential terms when they negotiate deals with local governments.[260]

For a technology company such as Huawei, moving into a new market can be expensive—a problem alleviated by government subsidies that make Huawei's products significantly cheaper than its competitors and Chinese financing to Huawei's customers that enables them to purchase these already cheaper products at lower interest rates with more generous grace periods. Once Huawei is in place, it is relatively cheaper for additional Chinese companies to follow it into that market or for Huawei to gain a foothold in adjacent markets.[261]

China often offers BRI countries complete technology packages, including cloud services, mobile payments, smart cities, and social media applications from a combination of Chinese companies.[262] Once these technology suites are embedded, switching to non-Chinese providers becomes far less likely and more costly for local operators, especially because telecommunications companies generally cannot mix and match components—using Huawei equipment alongside

Figure 11. HUAWEI'S 5G NETWORKS SUPPORT CHINA'S AMBITIONS, WHILE BANS THREATEN TO DERAIL THEM

Official approaches to using Huawei equipment in 5G networks

● Using or planning to use   ● Unlikely to use   ● Restrictions   ● Banned
○ Not yet considering 5G or no data

Source: CFR research.

Ericsson or Nokia, for example. Moreover, if Huawei builds the entire 5G network for a given DSR country and its neighbors, this raises the chances that it will be chosen to upgrade those systems when newer technologies become available.[263] Huawei has already finalized more 5G contracts than any other telecom company, half of which are for 5G networks in Europe (see figure 11).[264] In Africa, Huawei has built 70 percent of the fourth-generation (4G) networks on the continent and has signed the only formal agreement on 5G on the continent.[265]

In all, Huawei has shipped seventy thousand 5G base stations globally.[266] The export of Huawei telecom equipment along the DSR has also enabled the company's share of global telecom equipment to increase by 40 percent in the years since BRI was rolled out.[267] China's Belt and Road Portal reports DSR has enabled six thousand Chinese internet companies and more than ten thousand Chinese technology products to enter foreign markets.[268]

Huawei's penetration of BRI countries is concerning for the United States, which assesses that the company is effectively an extension of the CCP. Under China's 2017 National Intelligence Law, Huawei, like all Chinese technology companies, is legally required to conduct intelligence work on behalf of the Chinese government.[269] According to this analysis, the Chinese government has the ability to use Huawei-built 5G networks to collect intelligence, monitor critics, steal intellectual property, and disable networks.

DSR provides additional backing to Chinese companies to build foreign digital ecosystems.[270] Alibaba, the Chinese e-commerce giant, has come to dominate e-commerce in Malaysia, for example, and its affiliate Ant Financial has subsequently established cooperation agreements with Malaysian banks, leading to much stronger bilateral commercial and financial ties.[271] Malaysia is an outlier in the extent of its embrace of Chinese e-commerce, but the Chinese government has also begun a push to export data centers, including through ASEAN, which could make members depend more on China for data storage, analysis, and exploitation.[272]

Through DSR, China uses the initial sales of digital infrastructure to set accompanying standards. The success of Chinese companies such as Huawei and ZTE in building 5G networks and setting standards for these networks in Africa and parts of Asia is making it difficult for Western companies to sell similar technologies in these regions.[273] The concern for non-Chinese firms is China's ability to use initial sales, along with service and maintenance contracts—and any accompanying standards—to lock in market share for Chinese companies, particularly in those sectors where switching to a different provider is difficult and expensive.

BRI will give China additional tools to exploit mass quantities of data.

By providing Chinese companies with massive amounts of data, DSR will enhance China's global collection capabilities. This is all the more true because DSR helps Chinese companies export new technologies in bundles, such as smart cities, smart ports, and 5G-based AI and data analytics products that travel together.[274] Chinese companies sell smart ports, for example, which are intended to create efficiencies in unloading and productivity using sensors and automated functions, rather than simply constructing the port or offering discrete products to service it.[275] But technological bundling also allows for massive data processing and extraction. 5G technology allows for data collection and centralization, while AI allows for its processing and exploitation.[276]

Historically, the United States has itself pressed U.S. telecommunications companies to gain intelligence advantages, within legal bounds and not for commercial advantage. Whether because of SOEs' roles in building global digital infrastructure or because of enduring fears that the Chinese government can access data held by private firms, China's digital footprint has radically transformed its own ability to collect, process, and exploit the data of DSR countries and their neighbors. This data is likely to be primarily commercial and financial, and its quality is unknown. But even financial data can be used to political effect, and some Chinese projects are highly sensitive, such as the building of undersea cables.

China could use the data extracted for the gain of Chinese firms or to hinder market access for foreign companies; to coerce or manipulate political elites abroad; or to spy on foreign governments or military facilities, including on U.S. allies or near U.S. bases.[277] Furthermore, the massive quantities of data accrued from China's control over internet networks will put the country in a position to conduct espionage more effectively and even to improve its offensive cyber operations.[278]

China uses BRI to establish its preferred technical standards, including those for 5G networks.

Technical standards—that is, the regulations and protocols that govern using a repeatable technical task—can be set through two routes. One is through global standards bodies, such as the International Organization for Standardization (ISO), the International Electrotechnical Commission (IEC), and the International Telecommunications Union (ITU), in which China is among the best-represented members.[279] The other is through market volume; by dominating a market, China could implicitly win support for its preferred standards across a range of technologies, including 5G and AI.

China's Action Plan for Standards Connectivity for the Joint Construction of the Belt and Road calls for uniform technical standards across BRI. At the 2017 Belt and Road Forum, China signed agreements on mutual standard recognition with twelve countries, including Cambodia, Greece, Malaysia, Russia, and Switzerland. As of 2019, eighty-five such agreements had been signed with forty-nine countries and regions. By incorporating technical standards into BRI-related MOUs, China could win support for its preferred standards through project negotiations, as well as gain the political support of DSR countries in standard-setting bodies.[280]

For example, China is well positioned to influence standards for 5G technology, which promises data speeds twenty times faster than current telecom networks, and on which so many other technologies will depend. The ITU, including its secretary-general, is populated by current and former Chinese telecom officials. Senior Chinese officials have made clear that they expect Chinese nationals serving at the ITU to push China's preferred standards and promote the adoption of Huawei technology.[281] Huawei receives substantial government support for these efforts and currently has a team of four hundred employees working full time on standardization contributions.[282]

China submitted more technical documents related to wired communication specifications to the ITU in 2019 than any other country, and its companies have already gained 10 percent of the 1,450 essential patents for 5G standards (in comparison, 46.1 percent are held by U.S. companies).[283] Huawei alone has filed 19,473 technical contributions to 5G standard setting, whereas Qualcomm—the largest U.S. contributor—has filed only 1,994.[284]

DSR will not, however, ineluctably promote Chinese technical standards. Where a given project involves partnership between a Chinese company and a European one, for example, or if a Chinese firm builds only a small part of a larger network, the international standard could well prevail. But where DSR contracts are awarded exclusively to Chinese firms, as is true in most cases, Chinese technical standards will likely prevail. China has begun to promote its preferred standards in a variety of industries, including, but not limited to, new technologies, through BRI.[285]

Global Health

China is rebranding BRI for the global health crisis.

Early in the COVID-19 pandemic, the Chinese government resurrected a mothballed Health Silk Road moniker designed to rhetorically extend BRI to encompass China's vision of global health governance. The concept dates back to a 2015 Chinese health official's proposal to enhance international health cooperation under BRI's "people-to-people exchange" component.[286] Then, in January 2017, Xi Jinping visited the World Health Organization (WHO) in Geneva, where an official BRI MOU was signed supporting a Health Silk Road to establish a system to contain disease outbreaks, achieve a "community of common health for mankind," and improve public health outcomes in BRI countries.[287]

Chinese officials have continued to invoke the HSR as Beijing has sought to build a positive diplomatic narrative around its sale and donation of medical supplies to COVID-19–stricken countries and receive recognition as a leader in global health. In May, Xi addressed the World Health Assembly and announced a series of Chinese measures to address the pandemic, starting with $2 billion in aid to hard-hit countries. China's plans also include the establishment of a response hub in China in conjunction with the WHO, a cooperative arrangement pairing African and Chinese hospitals, and pledges to ensure that any vaccine developed would be treated as a "global public product."[288] The HSR is one indicator of a broader Chinese push to continue pursuing its vision for a global governance system, even amid a catastrophic international crisis.[289]

The COVID-19 pandemic and the promotion of the HSR could also incentivize Chinese companies to export health-related technological platforms to BRI countries, particularly diagnostic systems and digital health-monitoring tools.[290] China's efforts at combating COVID-19 have featured everything from use of its 5G networks to connect frontline workers and patients in remote locations to medical experts in Beijing, to robots' taking patients' vital measurements and drone deliveries of PPE, all supporting China's drive for a technology-empowered global health system.[291] Already China has offered AI-powered diagnostic technology to a few of its BRI partners and promoted 5G-based networks for the provision of remote health care.[292] Huawei is offering cloud systems to store health data and hospital databases online.[293]

Although there are some limits to China's ability to export its technological platforms, particularly its digital contact tracing systems, as many BRI countries lack the capacity to implement such systems, the shift to providing digital health-care technology allows Beijing to keep BRI alive and of critical importance to a number of countries.

China is using the HSR to rebuild its reputation on the international stage.

One of China's objectives in promoting the HSR and its "community of common health" is to shape the narrative about its role in the pandemic. Blamed worldwide for initially withholding information about the virus outbreak in Wuhan and for pressuring the WHO to praise China while holding back on declaring a Public Health Emergency of International Concern, China has sought to use its health diplomacy to shift the story away from China as the epicenter of the pandemic to one of Chinese contributions to addressing the problem.[294]

Starting in March 2020, China began a campaign of "mask diplomacy" to provide PPE and testing kits to its BRI partners and others around the world.[295] Chinese companies joined the efforts, with the Jack Ma Foundation donating more than two hundred million units of PPE, testing kits, and ventilators to more than 150 countries.[296]

Beijing dispatched medical teams to treat patients in numerous BRI countries and used its embassies to provide bilateral consultations on best practices for fighting COVID-19.[297] It extended a $500 million loan to Sri Lanka and sent a team of experts to Bangladesh, both prominent BRI countries, to train medical professionals.[298] Xi pledged to make a COVID-19 vaccine "a global public good" available to all, only more recently adding the caveat "at a fair and reasonable price" to his offer.[299]

China also worked to enhance its role as a leader on global health issues. When the United States announced its withdrawal from the WHO in July 2020, China stepped up its contributions to the organization and increasingly relied on its growing clout within the WHO to project its ability to both lead and collaborate with others in the fight against the coronavirus. China played a coordinating role in multilateral forums to champion China's international response to COVID-19. Chinese representatives have worked with ASEAN, the Shanghai Cooperation Organization, the Central and Eastern European 17+1 mechanism, and the African Union to ensure knowledge of best practices to combat the virus but also to tout Chinese success.[300]

China's effort to use the HSR and its mask diplomacy campaign to convince the world that it is a reliable and experienced global health partner has, however, had mixed success. A number of countries bristle at China's demand for public praise of its generosity. Italy, for example, ended up paying under a commercial contract for the majority of the masks, ventilators, and other medical equipment it received from China and, in the end, received far more in donations from European countries.[301] In addition, a growing list of complaints about faulty Chinese medical equipment and testing kits has marred the country's reputation and underscored concerns over quality controls in China.[302]

BRI partners closely aligned with Beijing, on the other hand, have been more willing to give China the praise it seeks, with Pakistan sending its president to China at the peak of the pandemic to show gratitude, Serbian President Alexander Vucic kissing the Chinese flag in appreciation, and billboards in Belgrade thanking "Brother Xi" for his help.[303]

China can be expected to tighten its quality controls and continue to provide significant amounts of medical supplies and PPE to the world, so its mask diplomacy could ultimately meet with greater success in repairing its reputation and further pulling BRI countries into its sphere of influence.

China's role as the world's largest supplier of medical goods allows it to deepen commercial ties.

The COVID-19 pandemic highlighted the degree to which the world relies on China for many critical medical supplies, PPE, active pharmaceutical ingredients, biotechnology products, and medical devices. Following the initial outbreak of the disease, China's need to provide medical goods to its own citizens led to considerable concerns over shortages and increased costs in the rest of the world. Beijing imposed restrictions on exports and bought up foreign producers, thereby ensuring control over domestic supply and future dominance of worldwide production of PPE and other medical supplies.[304] Even before the pandemic, China was the world's largest exporter of surgical masks, protective clothing, medical goggles, and respirators, along with active pharmaceutical ingredients.[305] In 2020, China exported 224 billion masks, enough to provide nearly 40 masks to every person living outside of China.[306]

This dependence on China leaves countries vulnerable to a Chinese decision to stop exporting its medicines and their crucial ingredients and raw materials, which could lead to shortages.[307] China could also use the world's need for its supply to bolster dependence on trade networks with China, while using BRI partner countries as additional incubators for Chinese health-care systems and technology.[308]

Even before the COVID-19 outbreak, China used the world's demand for its medical goods to ramp up investment in and production of a broad array of medical supplies, biotechnology products, PPE, and pharmaceuticals.[309] The sheer volume of production in China across the entire array of goods needed to fight the pandemic, along with substantial support from the government, has allowed Chinese companies to offer lower-cost products to its BRI partners. Because it manufactures so many medical supplies, China is likely to deepen commercial ties between Chinese medical, pharmaceutical, and PPE suppliers and BRI countries.

> The HSR could decrease global reliance on U.S. leadership and expertise in global health.

The HSR could have significant implications for U.S. interests. It highlights a need for the United States to reinvest in its own health infrastructure while deepening its commitment to global health efforts. The United States has long held a policy of providing resources to improve public health outcomes in low- and middle-income countries around the world.[310]

The United States is currently the world's largest donor to global health, and its investment has grown significantly over time. U.S. foundations, particularly the Bill and Melinda Gates Foundation, have also been major investors in global health, leaving the United States with a strong reputation as a reliable partner in the health-care fight. Since fiscal year (FY) 2010, however, U.S. funding for global health has remained relatively flat, and the Donald J. Trump administration proposed significant funding reductions for FY 2020.[311] In April 2020, the Trump administration went a step further by announcing that the United States would halt funding for the WHO, followed by a May 2020 declaration of the termination of the U.S. relationship with the organization.[312]

These reductions in support and participation create a vacuum that China has been filling with its well-funded effort to assist its BRI partners in addressing their health-care needs. However, China's ability to dominate the field of global health is limited. For example, China has not historically had a comparative advantage in offering on-the-ground international health training and is unlikely to develop it now.

Recent Chinese overtures during the COVID-19 pandemic have been amplified by the relative failure of the United States to adequately contain the virus at home, much less assume a global leadership role during the crisis. In addition to withdrawing from the WHO, the United States put export controls on PPE, thereby cutting off supplies to a number of countries in need.[313] On top of the cuts in federal funding for global health, the Trump administration redirected foreign aid and some of the work of the Development Finance Corporation (DFC) toward domestic efforts to secure supplies of PPE and other medical supplies rather than helping poor countries in need.[314] Although China joined COVAX—the vaccine partnership that aims to ensure equitable distribution of the COVID-19 vaccine and the provision of subsidized vaccines to poorer countries—the United States initially refused to do so. The Biden administration has indicated it will join COVAX, but, as of January 2021, the specific contours of its participation in that effort have yet to be defined.[315]

To its credit, however, the DFC recently announced a new Health and Prosperity Initiative, which includes a proposed $2 billion in support for health-related investments in developing countries.[316] This effort, if backed with sufficient resources, could allow the United States to regain some of its lost influence. In addition, the United States' successful development of three vaccines for COVID-19 and its mass vaccination efforts underway could help rebuild soft power through demonstrated expertise in marshaling resources to so quickly produce the vaccines, demonstrate the innovative capacities of U.S. companies, and better position the country to compete with China in projecting international influence in the health realm.

For its part, China has begun prioritizing its partner BRI countries for vaccine distribution, promising free vaccines across Africa and Southeast Asia, announcing $1 billion in loans to help Latin American and Caribbean countries purchase vaccines, and pledging one hundred thousand free doses to Bangladesh.[317] For at least sixteen countries, China's promise to provide vaccines was made in exchange for help with carrying out vaccine trials, given the low number of COVID-19–infected candidates for testing in China.[318] Although most of these countries were grateful for the partnership, others have raised concerns over whether they are being used as human guinea pigs in support of Chinese pharmaceutical companies.[319] These collaborations made it possible for China's fifth vaccine candidate to enter its final, third-phase clinical trials as of December 2020, with mid-September marking the first foreign approval, by the United Arab Emirates, of one of China's earlier vaccines.[320]

China has demanded public statements of gratitude for its efforts and in some instances sought more than just thanks for the provision of its vaccines to others. When Philippines President Rodrigo Duterte pled for access to Chinese vaccines, he reiterated that the Philippines would not confront Beijing over its South China Sea claims or host U.S. military bases.[321]

Beijing's vaccine diplomacy presents far more significant opportunities than its mask diplomacy, potentially allowing China to become the undisputed health-care supplier to the developing world provided things go well with its vaccines. Although twenty-four countries have signed deals to acquire Chinese vaccines, some political and medical leaders in these nations have voiced concerns about their quality and efficacy. Left unaddressed, these concerns could create lasting reputational costs for China. In addition, Beijing could also face trade-offs between the need to vaccinate its population and its vaccine diplomacy, as its capacity to manufacture vaccines will likely fall short of demand.[322]

Either way, the U.S. withdrawal from providing global health leadership gives China numerous ways to use its HSR to reframe the narrative about the pandemic, to shore up long-term markets for its producers of medical goods, PPE, pharmaceuticals, and health-care technology, and to assert itself as the leader in providing health care to the developing world.

The U.S. Response to BRI

> The United States has become increasingly critical of BRI, but its blanket condemnation risks alienating partners.

When Xi Jinping announced BRI, the Obama administration was well into its second term and executing its "pivot" or "rebalance" to Asia. At the time, BRI lacked its present geographic breadth and multi-domain security significance. The United States and China were simultaneously competing in areas such as the South China Sea and cooperating on more transnational issues than they are today. Debt crises along the Belt and Road had yet to emerge, and China had not yet taken control of strategic assets, such as the Hambantota Port, or so explicitly used the economic leverage provided by BRI to coerce host countries.

To most analysts, it was not clear that BRI put U.S. interests at risk. The United States viewed cooperation with China to address the North Korean nuclear threat, negotiate an end to Iran's nuclear ambitions, and bring the world together under the Paris Climate Accords as legitimate affirmative objectives. As a result, the U.S.-China bilateral relationship reflected the transnational issues at stake, and the administration took a more hands-off approach to BRI.

Although the Obama administration did not formally articulate a position on BRI, its perspective was evident in efforts to conclude negotiations for the Trans-Pacific Partnership (TPP, now known as the Comprehensive and Progressive Agreement for Trans-Pacific Partnership, or CPTPP), which would have formed a trade block representing 40 percent of global output, made the United States more economically competitive in Asia, and put pressure on China to raise its standards.

The Obama administration also made smaller commitments to connecting and investing in the Indo-Pacific and launched its Power Africa public-private partnership to electrify Africa.[323] It created a Global Procurement Initiative at the U.S. Trade and Development Agency (USTDA) to provide developing countries with a tool kit for more open and transparent procurement practices, better methods to determine fair value for purchases, and assistance in selecting smarter and more sustainable infrastructure.[324]

Not wanting to impede efforts to fill sizable investment gaps in Asia, Obama and other senior administration officials instead stressed the importance of ensuring high transparency and governance standards across Chinese initiatives, including BRI and AIIB.[325] They feared, as Obama explained in making the case for TPP, that "if we don't write the rules, China will write the rules."[326] Ultimately, BRI received modest policy attention in its first few years under the Obama administration, even as senior officials made public and private efforts to encourage sustainable and transparent economic practices across a set of Chinese bilateral and multilateral projects.

The Trump administration, faced with a BRI that had gone global, Chinese efforts to use BRI to set international standards and establish a foothold for the spread of Chinese-controlled digital technologies, and evidence that many of its projects were not economically sustainable, was blunt about its efforts to counter BRI. The United States employed a range of tools to do so, including publicly raising flags about harmful elements of BRI, redesigning U.S. government agencies to better compete with China on strategic infrastructure, working to mitigate the risks that Huawei and other Chinese technologies in BRI countries present to U.S. interests, and shining a light on bribery and corruption along BRI.

Over the past few years, senior officials have publicly warned countries about the risks of getting involved in BRI, mainly emphasizing the debt burden of BRI projects and China's use of BRI to increase its coercive leverage. U.S. Secretary of State Mike Pompeo accused China of using BRI to try to purchase an "empire" and vowed "to oppose them at every turn."[327] Addressing Asia-Pacific Economic Cooperation (APEC) members in 2018, Vice President Mike Pence warned countries, "Do not accept foreign debt that could compromise your sovereignty....The United States deals openly, fairly. We do not offer a constricting belt or a one-way road."[328] National Security Advisor John Bolton argued BRI had the "ultimate goal of advancing Chinese global dominance."[329] Admiral Philip Davidson, commander of U.S. Indo-Pacific Command, charged that BRI was "a stalking horse to advance Chinese security concerns."[330]

The U.S. response to BRI has been insufficient.

The United States has undertaken welcome initiatives to retool its government agencies to better compete with China in BRI countries. In October 2018, Trump signed into law the Better Utilization of Investments Leading to Development (BUILD) Act, which created the Development Finance Corporation (DFC) to replace the U.S. Overseas Private Investment Corporation (OPIC) as the country's official development bank. Sixty billion dollars, or twice as much money as OPIC had available to it, was provided to the DFC to invest in infrastructure projects in the developing world. The U.S. Agency for International Development (USAID)'s Development Credit Authority was also transferred to DFC, and the DFC was given additional authorities, such as the ability to do business with non-U.S. companies, take equity stakes in projects, and lend to SOEs.

The Trump administration hoped that these new authorities would allow the DFC to provide more flexible financing terms and, with the U.S. government as a partner, lower the political and regulatory risks for participation by the U.S. private sector. The intent was to provide a counterweight to China's state-centric BRI by catalyzing private capital and helping the private sector compete in frontier markets.

The United States has also sought to position the Export-Import Bank of the United States (U.S. EXIM) to better compete with China. In 2019, China provided official export credits totaling more than six times that offered by the United States, and over the past five years China's official export credit activity equaled 90 percent of that provided by all G7 countries combined.[331] Much of this financing went to BRI countries.

Recognizing the need to offer alternatives to BRI, in 2019 Congress passed a historic seven-year authorization for U.S. EXIM. Congress directed it to establish a "Program on China and Transformational Exports," which provides U.S. EXIM with the authority to offer lower rates and more flexible terms to compete with Chinese loans in high-tech sectors, including 5G, renewable energy, and fintech. Congress instructed U.S. EXIM to devote not less than 20 percent of its financing authority—$27 billion—to this program.[332] In December 2020, U.S. EXIM's board of directors voted to relax U.S. content requirements for companies to qualify for export financing in ten sectors identified in the Program on China and Transformational Exports, a welcome development that should help U.S. companies better compete with China along the Belt and Road.[333]

The United States, Australia, and Japan announced an effort to cofinance infrastructure in the Asia-Pacific. This trilateral initiative was followed by the unveiling in November 2019 of the Blue Dot Network (BDN), a body that would certify infrastructure projects around the world that have met high standards of governance, transparency, and developmental efficacy. The hope was that if a project received the Blue Dot seal of approval, private capital would have more confidence in it and be more likely to provide funding. Both DFC and BDN are attempts to incentivize U.S. pension and insurance funds to invest a percentage of the trillions of dollars they manage in infrastructure, which would present a serious alternative to BRI.[334] It is unclear, however, whether BDN has the resources to fulfill its mission; it is currently buried within the State Department's website, lacks dedicated staff to vet projects, and provides nowhere for an applicant to submit a project for review.[335]

Responding to BRI's inroads in the United States' own hemisphere, where the initiative has grown to include nineteen countries in Latin America and the Caribbean, the State Department unveiled Growth in the Americas (América Crece), which aims to promote private-sector investment in infrastructure in the region. Under this whole-of-government effort, the United States works with countries to improve their regulatory regimes in order to make them more attractive to U.S. investors, supports project financing, undertakes feasibility studies, and holds trade missions. So far, Argentina, Chile, Guyana, Jamaica, Panama, and Suriname have signed MOUs joining this initiative. At the same time, the program explicitly notes it "primarily leverages existing programs, diplomatic engagement, technical expertise, and partnerships to achieve initiative goals and objectives."[336]

In order to mitigate the perceived national security risks of Chinese-built 5G telecommunications infrastructure, the Trump administration leveraged the United States' dominance of advanced semiconductors, barring sales of essential computer chips to Huawei without a specific license.[337] Access to U.S. chips, particularly 5G-related semiconductors that enable wireless communications, network management, and data storage, is crucial to Huawei, which is reported to be running out of supply.[338] The administration, however, undercut the credibility of its national security argument when it made clear that it viewed these restrictions on sales to Huawei as a bargaining chip in trade negotiations with China.[339] In response, realizing how reliant its companies remain on U.S. technology, China has begun to redouble efforts to develop its indigenous industry and break the stranglehold. Should China successfully wean itself off U.S. semiconductors and develop its own alternative, the United States would lose a significant source of leverage that it could employ during a potential crisis.

Recognizing the DSR's potential to entrench Chinese technology companies in the critical infrastructure of BRI countries, the Trump administration pressured countries not to use Chinese components in their 5G infrastructure. In 2020, Secretary of State Pompeo announced a Clean Network initiative intended to promote data privacy and security along 5G networks. More than thirty carriers around the world have joined this initiative and pledged to exclude Chinese components in their 5G infrastructure.[340] This was later expanded to include a "Clean Cable" effort that aims to ensure China cannot compromise the information carried by undersea cables.[341]

The work of other government programs has taken on renewed urgency in light of BRI. USAID's Power Africa program, for example, has signed 124 power generation deals worth more than $22 billion, with forty-seven plants already operational.[342] Power Africa's private-public partnership approach of bringing together African partners, the private sector, NGOs, private capital, and multilateral donors stands in contrast to BRI's largely government-to-government, top-down approach. Similarly, the Commerce Department's Commercial Law and Development Program (CLDP) has shifted to efforts that indirectly respond to China's BRI activities. In Africa, CLDP is assisting Power Africa by encouraging African officials to insist on international best practices and terms in their energy and power purchase contracts. CLDP's efforts in Central Asia have focused on the development of transparent and accountable public procurement systems that will leave Central Asian governments better prepared when contracting with China. In Southeast Asia, work is concentrated in the energy sector and in developing transparent legal and procedural frameworks to oversee complex infrastructure projects.[343]

Although many of these policies and programs are welcome, the response to BRI has been too little, too late. The Trump administration's decision to eschew multilateralism and step back from the historic role the United States has played coordinating allies and partners in addressing shared challenges has also undermined the U.S. response to BRI. The Trump administration also undercut its own objectives, arguing countries should ban Huawei and ZTE on national security grounds but then agreeing that relief for Huawei could be a part of trade negotiations and lifting sanctions on ZTE because of "too many jobs in China lost."[344]

Ultimately, the scattershot U.S. response has failed to protect its interest in encouraging sustainable and inclusive development, maintaining fair access to overseas markets for U.S. goods and services, setting standards that will promote quality digital and hard infrastructure, and ensuring macroeconomic stability and growth.

RECOMMENDATIONS

The Task Force recommends that the United States implement policies aimed at lowering the macroeconomic risk of BRI, providing alternatives to BRI, increasing digital choices in the developing world, and upholding high environmental standards.

In order to pursue these objectives, the United States has to mitigate the risks to countries receiving Chinese loans, improve its competitiveness, coordinate with allies and partners to meet the needs of developing countries in responsible and sustainable ways, and protect U.S. security interests along the Belt and Road.

Mitigate Economic Risks of BRI

BRI has demonstrated its ability to saddle countries with unsustainable debt, displace U.S. companies from emerging markets by tilting the playing field in favor of Chinese firms, push countries to adopt technical standards that are not compatible with U.S. products, and spread corruption through its opaque financing.

The United States should address each of these concerns in order to ensure its companies remain globally competitive and to promote global macroeconomic stability. The COVID-19 crisis has made the issue of debt sustainability a more immediate concern, and heading off debt crises in BRI countries should be a priority of the United States.

> Lead a global effort to mitigate the effects of an emerging debt crisis.

The United States should lead efforts to extend a full debt repayment moratorium for low-income countries through the end of 2021 and consider more far-reaching debt relief initiatives if needed. Extending the G20 debt freeze to the end of 2021 could make available an estimated $50 billion for domestic spending to combat COVID-19 within the seventy-six International Development Association (IDA) countries.[345]

The United States should work to ensure that China lives up to its responsibilities by treating BRI-related claims as official debt and subject to generous restructuring terms in line with other official creditors.

To facilitate effective and coordinated responses to debt problems in the future, the United States should work to bring China into the Paris Club, an informal group of twenty-two of the largest official creditors that work together to coordinate approaches to countries experiencing debt distress.

Partner with other countries to demand that China publish official data on its overseas lending.

In order to provide reliable macroeconomic oversight, the IMF, World Bank, G20, and large creditors need a shared understanding of how much the most vulnerable countries owe and on what terms. China's opaque lending practices, however, distort debt sustainability analysis and impair economic surveillance.

Although members of the Organization for Economic Cooperation and Development (OECD) and Paris Club are required to report their official loans, China is not a member of these organizations, and as a result its lending is not published. CDB and China EXIM do not report the terms of their loans, and China has not published an official foreign aid report since 2014.[346] Estimates of its overseas lending therefore vary by orders of magnitude.[347] One recent study analyzed five thousand Chinese loans totaling $520 billion and found that as much as half of the country's lending to developing countries is not reported to the World Bank or IMF.[348]

China pushes BRI countries to keep their books closed and only discuss renegotiations with China on a bilateral basis. The United States and its partners should insist that China report its loans.

Promote U.S. companies in the face of unfair Chinese competition, educate foreign governments on the advantages of working with U.S. firms, and raise awareness among publics of the risks of BRI.

Raising awareness of the benefits of partnering with U.S. firms requires a robust set of U.S. institutions dedicated to that goal. The U.S. government should bolster its ability to conduct economic and commercial advocacy for U.S. companies through partnership with the private sector and bilateral coordination with BRI host countries.

U.S. ambassadors to BRI countries should be advised through their presidential letter of instruction to seek opportunities for U.S. companies to compete against BRI investments from China.

U.S. embassies should be tasked with helping governments in BRI countries understand that, though China could offer faster or cheaper infrastructure projects, factors such as environmental impact mitigation, the transfer of skills and knowledge to local workforces, and transparency in terms, financial sustainability, product quality, and longevity are far more important in the long run and that U.S. firms could be better partners.

To further assist U.S. commercial efforts in BRI countries, the United States should ensure the Foreign Commercial Service is fully supported in its mission, including by staffing all global markets positions, especially its digital attachés and officials at the deputy assistant secretary level and above.

A fully staffed International Trade Administration should organize a set of trade missions, including executive-led ones, in BRI nations, targeting competition for projects and exports typical to BRI but consistent with other U.S. goals and standards.[349]

Further, the Departments of Commerce and State should jointly convene an advisory group consisting of representatives from academia, development organizations, and significant private-sector actors, including infrastructure construction companies, to facilitate the exchange of information on commercial opportunities and conditions around BRI, which can then be shared and applied to the benefit of U.S. commercial interests. The advisory group should include representation from U.S. EXIM and DFC to ensure awareness of available financial support for qualifying deals.

As part of this effort, the United States should support civil society actors in BRI countries to empower them to gain and disseminate information about the pros and cons of working with China on BRI projects and to ensure their capacity to provide input to impact assessments and to take advantage of grievance mechanisms.

To do so, the United States should devote more resources to funding investigative journalism and civil society in BRI countries, with the aim of providing tools to people that allow them to look into BRI's lending terms, environmental and economic sustainability, forced displacement of populations, and corruption.

> Offer technical support to BRI countries to help them vet prospective projects for economic and environmental sustainability.

The 2015 Addis Ababa Action Agenda recognized that developing countries often lack the technical expertise needed to evaluate infrastructure projects, determine debt sustainability, and navigate dispute resolution processes.[350] BRI has made this issue more pressing, as countries find themselves saddled with projects that will never pay for themselves and loaded with debt they cannot repay because they did not have the technical capabilities needed to scrutinize prospective projects.

In order to reduce the likelihood that future BRI projects will be white elephants, the United States should offer technical assistance to BRI countries by expanding the Department of Commerce's Infrastructure Transaction and Assistance Network and enlarging the Department of the Treasury's Office of Technical Assistance, including sending analysts to BRI countries to work with them on conducting macroeconomic assessments of projects.

The creation of the Transaction Advisory Fund (TAF) within the Department of State is a welcome initiative and has already proven successful in helping BRI countries negotiate more favorable contracts with China; indeed, with the help of U.S. economists, diplomats, and lawyers, Myanmar was able to negotiate the cost of the Kyaukpyu port down from $7.3 billion to $1.3 billon.[351] TAF's funding, which stands at $10 million, should be doubled in order to allow for more comprehensive assessment of a greater number of projects.

The United States should also work through the IMF and World Bank to strengthen their analytical tools for assessing debt sustainability and encourage BRI countries to adopt this framework for all projects. In every instance, it is imperative that the United States become involved early in the planning phase, as the ability of countries to change course and get out from under bad projects rapidly diminishes as projects progress.

In addition to helping BRI countries vet individual projects, the United States should assist them in setting up their own national screening mechanisms for evaluating Chinese infrastructure investments and associated security risks. This can include collaborating with the World Bank's International Finance Corporation and the OECD to assist BRI countries in developing the legal infrastructure and human resources needed to conduct robust investment screening.

The common investment criteria should guard against "corrosive capital" that lacks transparency, accountability, and market orientation.[352] It should set high standards around sustainability, financial viability, transparency, and labor standards and could build upon the OECD's FDI Qualities Indicators but also include specific criteria related to protections against cyber theft and using technology to enhance authoritarian regimes.[353]

Embark on a robust anticorruption campaign.

The United States should leverage the global reach of its laws, programs, and influence in a coordinated, global anticorruption campaign, including fighting BRI-related corruption, amplifying host country government and civil society efforts at reform, and advocating for more transparent procurement and bidding practices.

To that end, the United States should prioritize and cultivate international support, including through renewed commitment to the Open Government Partnership and increased support for USTDA's Global Procurement Initiative. Such efforts should be integrated into its diplomatic agenda; all U.S. ambassadors should be instructed to promote anticorruption principles and fair business practices, especially in BRI nations.

The United States should also fill critical State Department roles with responsibilities related to fighting corruption, including the undersecretary for civilian security, democracy, and human rights, with permanent, Senate-confirmed appointees, and create a new special representative for combatting corruption empowered to convene experts and decision-makers across functional and regional groups.[354] Further, the Department of State and USAID should cultivate internal anticorruption expertise and provide surge technical and political support to local embassies as needed.

The United States should also increase resources dedicated to the Department of Justice's prosecution of Foreign Corrupt Practices Act (FCPA) violations, including by non-U.S. individuals and corporations.[355] Further, Congress should pass proposed legislation to direct funds collected from FCPA enforcement to a new Anticorruption Action Fund, to augment rigid and limited existing anticorruption funding.[356]

Finally, the United States should better integrate the Commercial Law Development Program into cross-government anticorruption efforts, both existing and newly created, particularly those aimed at BRI nations.

Improve U.S. Competitiveness

The U.S. approach to BRI should focus on U.S. strengths. U.S. free-market principles, an innovative private sector, deep pools of private capital, leading educational institutions, a commitment to the rule of law, and a historical openness to immigration have nurtured the world's most innovative economy.

High domestic standards for quality, reliability, and transparency have led to companies known around the world for delivering results beneficial to host countries, along with the production of excellent goods and the delivery of first-rate services. Relatively open markets in much of the world have allowed highly competitive U.S. companies to establish a global presence. These advantages, however, are in danger of eroding.

As China closes the innovation gap with the United States and surpasses it in areas such as electronic payment systems, high-speed rail, and 5G, the United States is in danger of offering equal or inferior products while demanding higher standards—a losing combination. Improving U.S. competitiveness is essential to addressing BRI.

Boost federal funding for research and development.

To be competitive in international markets, the United States will need to continue to generate the world's leading technologies, and, to do this, it has to increase investments in R&D, as China is doing. This is even more important for technologies such as AI, where first-mover advantages quickly establish dominant winners. Federally funded research contributed to the development of the internet, touch screens, the Global Positioning System (GPS), advanced battery technology, and light-emitting diode (LED) technology, among others.

The federal government is able to make investments that are too big and risky for the private sector to undertake, and public R&D incentivizes greater R&D funding in the private sector. As a result, federal funding for R&D is a critical tool to foster innovation.

To retain an innovation edge over China, the U.S. government should

- boost federal funding for R&D from 0.7 percent to its historical average of 1.1 percent of GDP, devoting roughly $100 billion in additional spending on R&D annually;[357]

- direct some R&D funding to emerging digital technologies, such as AI, quantum computing, and next-generation telecommunications, which could be channeled through the Department of Energy's national laboratories;

- invest in universities to support cutting-edge research, which is even more urgent given that universities will likely have to cut funding to various programs because of budget shortfalls caused by COVID-19; and

- make additional investments in basic science, technology, engineering, and mathematics (STEM) education at all levels.

Increase investments in next-generation technologies, such as AI, 6G, clean energy, and health-care technology.

The United States led the world in rolling out a 4G long-term evolution (LTE) network, which provided U.S. companies with a significant first-mover advantage, enabling them to build applications and services that utilized this bandwidth and become dominant in wireless services. Leadership in LTE drove an expansion in the U.S. wireless industry, generating jobs and increasing U.S. GDP.[358]

As the world worked to develop the next generation of wireless networks—5G, which promises to offer speeds twenty times faster than 4G LTE—the United States abdicated its leadership role. The United States does not and will not have a company that is competitive in the full stack of 5G equipment, despite the critical role that 5G will play as the backbone for AI, automated vehicles, and the Internet of Things.

Countries around the world building their 5G infrastructure have only five companies to choose from: Ericsson, Huawei, Nokia, Samsung, and ZTE. This outcome is the result of a series of regulatory (primarily spectrum availability), tax, investment, research, and trade decisions that left the United States unprepared to compete in the next generation of communications technology.[359] Because of China's dominance in 5G, its companies will be the first to roll out the next generation of wireless services and applications, forcing U.S. companies to play catch-up.

This could happen again in other areas of technology and should serve as a wakeup call. A U.S. failure to lead in the competition to develop AI and the technical standards and norms surrounding it would be a much more significant setback than its failure to develop 5G, as AI promises to underpin innovation in an array of fields as diverse as biotechnology and national defense.[360]

To maintain its leadership role in innovation and technology development, the United States should

- make additional, significant investments in emerging technologies, particularly AI, quantum computing, advanced semiconductors, advanced battery storage, and 6G;

- prioritize high-risk, years-long investments that the private sector is often unable to finance (China invested $180 billion over five years to cement its leadership in 5G, and investment at a similar scale is needed to lead the race to 6G);[361]

- fund R&D centers at universities that focus on 6G technologies, which are likely to replace 5G within fifteen years;

- devote more attention to integrating its investments in next-generation technologies, with Congress playing a leadership role by appropriating resources for this effort;

- expand Power Africa's Clean Energy Solutions Center to a global program, targeting assistance to developing countries to help them design and adopt policies and programs that support clean energy;

- increase support for sustainable energy funds investing in developing countries; and

- invest in health-care technologies to ensure that the United States maintains its leading role as a developer and provider of state-of-the-art medical devices and pharmaceuticals.

Attract and retain the most talented immigrants and foreign-born students.

The United States' historical openness to immigrants and ability to attract the world's best students, researchers, scientists, and engineers has traditionally been one of the country's enduring strengths. Immigrants are roughly twice as likely as native-born Americans to start a new business, and 60 percent of the country's largest technology companies were founded by immigrants or the children of immigrants.[362] Nearly 80 percent of graduate students in electrical engineering and computer science are foreign nationals.[363] Immigrants have been critical to the development of the U.S. semiconductor industry, helping to establish U.S. leadership in a critical field.[364]

Recent policies, however, have made it more difficult for students to study in the United States and remain in the country after graduation, yet the ability to work in the United States is what attracts top students and allows the United States to reap the benefits of their talent. Nearly 80 percent of foreign-born PhD students in AI stay in the United States for at least five years after graduating.[365] COVID-19 has also made international students more reticent about enrolling in U.S. schools, given that virtual education does not provide the full complement of experiences that draws international students to the United States. Increased restrictions on the movement of professionals into the United States has limited talent recruitment, with the Trump administration's limits on H-1B visas proving particularly counterproductive.

While the United States is closing its doors to top talent, China is trying to to recruit top foreign experts, offering generous bonuses and incentives to recruit scientists, among others.[366]

To maintain its competitiveness, the United States should

- revamp and revitalize its visa programs to make it clear that it welcomes foreign talent;

- raise the cap on H-1B visas, grant green cards to postgraduate degree holders, and ensure that students wishing to study in the United States have ready access to visas that allow them to stay in the United States for the duration of their studies, including postgraduate externship through codification and expansion of the Optional Practical Training program;[367] and

- better use its embassies overseas to promote research and study opportunities in the United States.

> Increase U.S. participation in international standards-setting bodies to ensure that standards meet the highest levels of security, quality, and sustainability and are not barriers to U.S. exports.

Whereas China develops its standards in a top-down process directed by the Standardization Administration of China with research from state-sponsored institutes, and Europe often develops its standards based exclusively on input from EU-based participants, the United States has traditionally relied on an industry-based, consensus-driven, voluntary, and open process.

The current industry-led U.S. process for setting standards should be maintained but strengthened through enhanced support from the U.S. government. Robust U.S. participation in the ISO, IEC, ITU, Codex Alimentarius, World Organization of Animal Health (OIE), and International Plant Protection Convention is critical to ensuring that any standards that are adopted, and the process for the development of such standards, reflects U.S. interests.

To facilitate greater U.S. participation, the National Institute of Standards and Technology (NIST) should provide grants to support U.S. companies, particularly SMEs, to participate in standardization processes, including personnel funding for the development, writing, and submission of technical comments; support for required entry participation fees; and funds for travel to standards-setting events.

The United States should allow private companies to write off such participation as R&D tax credits.

Ensuring U.S. private-sector participation is essential, particularly for technology and telecommunications standards, but recent decisions to place certain foreign companies and officials on blocked lists means representatives from U.S. companies could be unable to attend important meetings if an entity on the blocked entities list is also participating.[368]

The Department of Commerce should issue new guidance to clarify that its inclusion of standards in the advisory opinion accompanying the May 2019 notice adding Huawei to the U.S. Entity List does not preclude Americans from attending standards-setting meetings, even if Huawei officials could also be in attendance.[369]

In addition, direct U.S. government participation at meetings of standards bodies, which has often been hampered by intermittent funding and competing priorities, needs to be consistent and sustained:

- U.S. government participation in standards-setting processes should be prioritized and provided with steady funding.[370]

- Congress should encourage interagency coordination that brings together officials from the Departments of State, Commerce, Justice, Defense, as well as NIST and that consults regularly with U.S. industry, including the possible establishment of a formal interagency committee.[371]

- The process for providing input to support U.S. government participation should be streamlined, particularly for smaller firms, so that U.S. government officials can go to standards-setting meetings well prepared to promote and defend U.S. interests.

Being able to host standards-setting meetings also boosts the United States' chance to achieve standards based on its own input and data. The State Department should help facilitate the conduct of the

COUNCIL on
FOREIGN
RELATIONS

100

58 East 68th Street, New York, NY 10065
tel 212.434.9400   fax 212.434.9401   www.cfr.org

April 22, 2021

Mr. Joseph C. Hill
47 Richards Rd
Port Washington, NY 11050-3822

Dear Mr. Hill:

As co-chairs of the bipartisan CFR-sponsored Independent Task Force on China's Belt and Road Initiative, we are pleased to share with you a copy of the group's report, *China's Belt and Road: Implications for the United States.*

The Belt and Road Initiative (BRI), Chinese President Xi Jinping's signature foreign policy endeavor, has the potential to meet developing countries' needs and spur economic growth, but the reality is often otherwise. Unless the United States offers an effective alternative, China could reorient global trade networks, set technical standards that disadvantage non-Chinese companies, lock countries into carbon-intensive futures, increase its political influence over countries, and acquire power-projection capabilities for its military. The COVID-19 pandemic has made a U.S. response more urgent, as the global economic contraction has accelerated the reckoning with BRI-related debt.

The report proposes that the United States put forward an affirmative agenda by drawing on its strengths and coordinating with allies and partners to promote sustainable, secure, and environmentally responsible development. We hope you will find the report of interest.

Sincerely,

Jacob J. Lew and Gary Roughead
Task Force Chairs

standards-setting process on U.S. soil by streamlining the visa process for foreign participants, and should coordinate a standards strategy with U.S. allies and partners.[372]

Because many U.S. allies and partners share the United States' desire for technical standards that meet high standards of security, quality, sustainability, and protection of civil liberties and human rights, U.S. officials attending standards-setting meetings should work with allies and partners to encourage BRI countries to adopt international standards wherever they exist and to develop such high standards where they do not.

In addition, the United States should work with its partners to press for governance reforms in the ITU, such as banning sitting government officials from assuming leadership roles in the organization and limiting the number of senior positions that can be held by nationals from any single country.

The United States should also work with its partners to improve the diversity, transparency, and merit-based decision-making at the ITU and other international standards organizations.

Provide DFC and U.S. EXIM with additional authorities to allow them to better compete with China.

In order to better compete with Chinese offerings in BRI countries, the United States should further empower DFC and U.S. EXIM. The BUILD Act, which established DFC, prioritized providing support to low-income and lower-middle-income economies and placed restrictions on DFC assistance to upper-middle-income economies.[373] Recognizing that 30 percent of BRI participants are in the upper-middle-income bracket, the United States should lift this restriction and allow DFC to compete in these markets.

Multiple reforms should be made to U.S. EXIM to allow it to better compete with China's BRI offerings. U.S. EXIM's decision to relax U.S. content requirements for ten specific industries identified in its Program on China and Transformational Exports is a welcome development, as it recognizes that in a world of global value chains, U.S. content is not the best proxy for support of U.S. jobs. This new content policy should be broadened to cover all U.S. EXIM loans because the ten areas identified do not encompass every sector in which the United States should compete with China—for example, in nuclear energy and traditional infrastructure, such as ports. Congress should also provide at least $20 million in dedicated funding and an increase in staffing for the Program.

In addition to directly supporting U.S. companies' activity abroad, DFC and U.S. EXIM should also focus on collaborative efforts between the public and private sectors in the United States and in its allies and partners. Without a U.S. 5G alternative, DFC could partner with its counterparts in Finland, South Korea, and Sweden to cofinance Nokia, Samsung, and Ericsson in their quest to gain 5G market share. Similarly, DFC should join other development finance institutions from around the world in the Currency Exchange Fund (TCX), which provides a variety of financial instruments, including swaps and forward contracts, to minimize exchange-rate risks, thereby giving emerging economies the ability to continue borrowing funds in their local currency.[374]

By pooling both private- and public-sector funds, capacity, and expertise, a coalition would have the linguistic skills, cultural connections, technical expertise, and financial resources to invest strategically in those areas where coalition-financed and built infrastructure would serve as a superior alternative to Chinese projects. Specifically, DFC should provide developing countries with loans or loan guarantees for telecommunications equipment and financial assistance through USAID to incentivize countries to choose alternatives to Chinese technology where that technology poses a risk to national security.[375] DFC and U.S. EXIM should also follow the Power Africa model of bringing together technical and regulatory experts, private-sector capital and production capabilities, and NGOs to create a coalition to provide a clean-energy alternative to China's carbon-intensive power projects. DFC should seek additional partnerships similar to the one created by its late 2020 partnership with the Rockefeller Foundation, whereby the Rockefeller Foundation committed to providing $50 million to de-risk DFC's investments in renewable energy.[376] Such partnerships would enable DFC and U.S. EXIM to invest more of its funds in supporting technological transformation and sustainable infrastructure.

> Promote U.S. technological options in BRI countries by simplifying digital transformation.

Cloud computing represents the next generation of computing, shifting computing power away from computers and individual server rooms to cloud storage. Businesses that want to be competitive need to shift their processes to the cloud, a transition that holds promise but also risk. The cloud-computing provider can see all of the data stored on the cloud, and although U.S. companies are contractually obligated to view only metadata, the truth is that any cloud-computing provider has the technical capability to access individual data.

The danger is that Chinese cloud-computing providers—Alibaba, Huawei, and Tencent—that are already globally competitive can access and compromise data. This represents a potentially larger threat than 5G. Although the most capable cloud providers are U.S. companies—Amazon, HP, IBM, Microsoft, and Oracle, among others—Chinese companies are competent in this area and offer a cheaper option for developing countries.

In order to promote the adoption of U.S. products in this critical area, the United States should create a model that allows countries to have a simple, one-stop shop for cloud solutions. The United States should establish regional hubs in Africa, Latin America, and Southeast Asia, staffed with officials from U.S. EXIM, DFC, the Department of Commerce, and the Department of State, which can offer packages to regional governments and facilitate a competitive tender process for U.S. companies to bid. This effort would emphasize that the total cost of ownership a U.S. company can offer is competitive with its Chinese counterparts, particularly when a country factors in the software and management necessary to manage cloud computing.

Develop Partnerships and Strengthen Multilateral Organizations to Meet Developing Country Needs

A successful response to BRI should include U.S. allies and partners. In addition to making necessary domestic reforms to become more competitive with China's offering in BRI countries, the United States should deepen its multilateral partnerships and strengthen multilateral institutions. This includes ensuring that international financial institutions—including the World Bank, IMF, and regional development banks—have the resources and policies in place to meet the challenges, exacerbated by COVID-19, facing the developing world.

> Ensure that the IFIs have the resources and policies to meet the needs of developing countries.

In its earliest years, the World Bank primarily funded infrastructure, focusing on transportation, energy, and water projects. But in recent decades, it has moved away from financing infrastructure, particularly coal-fired power plants and other projects inconsistent with UN Sustainable Development Goals. As a result, and because World Bank funding is tied to requirements for transparency, high standards, environmental impact assessments, and sustainability that some developing countries find difficult to comply with, China has been able to capture much of the pent-up demand for roads, railways, ports, power, and technology.

The United States has a strong interest in offering an infrastructure program that promotes sustainable and inclusive development, sets high standards, enables U.S. firms to compete on a level playing field, and promotes macroeconomic growth and stability. Borrowing countries ultimately benefit from the higher standards, greater transparency, and a stronger commitment to sustainability present in lending from the World Bank and other MDBs. The planet is also better off from attention devoted to the environmental consequences of projects.

For these reasons, and despite its recent turn away from infrastructure, the World Bank and its related institutions remain the best alternative to BRI. Given its long history of leadership in the World Bank and its unique position in World Bank governance, the United States is well positioned to spearhead much-needed reforms to the institution.

In order to ensure the World Bank has sufficient resources, the United States should lead an international effort to increase its funding, particularly the IDA window for the poorest countries. Although the United States led a $13 billion paid-in capital increase in 2018, because of the economic catastrophe brought on by COVID-19, an additional capital increase is necessary.[377] In light of the concerns about debt sustainability, the focus should be on lending with high levels of concessionality.

In addition, the United States should contribute to the World Bank's Global Infrastructure Facility to ensure recipient countries get enough help with project financing, planning, and structuring at the outset of project development to allow them to make smart choices in favor of high-quality, sustainable, cost-effective infrastructure projects. During this process, the United States should work with partners to ensure that the World Bank's facilities are as responsive as possible to the needs of its borrowers.

The United States should also work to reorient the World Bank toward increased funding for digital connectivity, infrastructure, and energy access while emphasizing sustainable development, transparency, and promotion of the rule of law.

The United States should support the World Bank's collaborating with other multilateral lenders—including the Asian Infrastructure Investment Bank—as a way of strengthening international adherence to high lending standards.

The United States should ensure developing countries have a greater voice at the World Bank so they have more confidence that the World Bank understands their needs and is working to address them. It should also make sure the World Bank and IMF's Debt Management Facility is well equipped to offer training for government officials and technical assistance to countries to help them better manage their debt.

Finally, it would appear anomalous that China, which through BRI has become a major source of development finance, itself borrows from the World Bank. China is essentially borrowing at concessionary rates to fund its own domestic development priorities and then lending at higher rates to developing countries through BRI. The World Bank should assess the appropriateness of its policies that allow China to continue to borrow from it.

Work with allies and members of the BRI Green Development Coalition to insist that China live up to its Green Belt and Road pledges.

The potential for BRI to cause lasting damage to the environment and set back any chance to meet the Paris Accord pledges for reduction in greenhouse gas emissions can be avoided only through a concerted effort to hold China to its Green Belt and Road pledges.

Efforts should begin with requiring pre-project environmental assessments under both the "green, yellow, red" framework classification system recently crafted by the BRICG and by encouraging China to join the Espoo Convention, which requires parties to assess environmental impacts at an early stage of planning and to consult the other parties to the Convention on all major projects likely to have significant adverse environmental effects across boundaries.[378]

The United States and its partners should press China to establish strict regulations on the monitoring and financing of all BRI projects based on its BRIGC classification, while requiring a phase-out of any financing for red projects, starting with coal and other fossil fuel energy investments whose severe and irreversible damage cannot be mitigated.

Similarly, Beijing should be pushed to make the provision of an environmental impact assessment a prerequisite for insurance coverage from Sinosure or other Chinese insurance companies.[379]

China should be encouraged to adopt binding standards for what constitutes a green BRI investment so that clear, internationally recognized standards are applied rather than the status quo of counting anything that complies with local, often low-level, environmental standards as a green investment.

Beijing should be pressed to require its banks to adopt carbon-limiting lending standards consistent with either domestic Chinese standards or those of the MDBs, including the MDBs' 2019 Framework and Principles for Climate Resilience Metrics in Financing Operations.[380]

Chinese policy banks should also be required to follow the World Bank's lead in setting up environmental departments to oversee environmental assessments for all of their BRI lending.[381]

Finally, a transparent process to ensure compliance with Green Belt and Road pledges is essential. China should be encouraged to establish a compliance mechanism, potentially accompanied by inspectors in BRI countries, to assess adherence to the Green Investment Principles and China's Guidance on Promoting a Green Belt and Road.

Similarly, China's compliance with its own commendable pledge to achieve carbon neutrality before 2060 should be monitored, particularly to ensure that China does not achieve it by simply moving its coal-fired power and other high-carbon-emitting plants outside of its borders. Carbon emissions from such Chinese outsourced plants could be attributed to China rather than the host country.

Just as the United States began publishing data on air quality in Beijing, which helped prompt China to take this issue seriously, it should work with allies and partners to tabulate emissions of BRI projects and publicly report them.

> Reenergize the U.S.-led trade agenda to write the rules for the twenty-first-century global economy.

The United States should prioritize multilateral trade diplomacy in order to create a high-standards, rules-based alternative to Chinese-backed pacts, starting with the rules on digital trade, subsidies, and fintech:

- The United States should work to expand on the U.S.-Japan Digital Trade Agreement by bringing other countries into that agreement or negotiating comparable arrangements with other countries. Such an agreement would ensure nondiscriminatory treatment of digital products and cross-border data flows while establishing collaboration and supplier adherence to common principles to address cybersecurity.

- Additional efforts should be made to cooperate on maintaining a free and open internet that would link the U.S. economy and society to other open countries while protecting against China's misuse of the internet.

- The United States should prioritize finishing the U.S.-EU-Japan trilateral project to develop new disciplines on subsidies and the coerced transfer of technology.

- The United States should continue to press China and its BRI partners to open their markets to foreign competition, both in bilateral negotiations and by joining with allies at the WTO, APEC, and other multilateral forums.

- The United States should work within the G7, G20, and the Financial Stability Board to develop standards and protocols to monitor and safeguard financial technology, including developing risk-assessment standards.

All of these efforts represent a U.S.-led alternative to RCEP, an opportunity to create high-standards agreements, and the most viable way to give U.S. technology companies a better chance to compete in BRI markets.

Second, the United States should work to improve and then join the Comprehensive and Progressive Agreement for Trans-Pacific Partnership. CPTPP currently provides tariff preferences, binding commitments on access to services markets, rules on digital trade and intellectual property protections, restrictions on state-owned enterprises, requirements for domestic adoption of internationally agreed-upon labor and environmental commitments, and a strong dispute settlement system applicable to trade among its eleven members (Australia, Brunei, Canada, Chile, Japan, Malaysia, Mexico, New Zealand, Peru, Singapore, and Vietnam), seven of which have signed on to BRI.

By reopening negotiations to join CPTPP, the United States would signal to those seven BRI countries that they should remain committed to trade and investment with the United States on terms that are more favorable than with China and are grounded in a cooperative, rules-based system.

Signaling an interest in joining the CPTPP could be accompanied by indications of changes the United States is likely to seek, including improved labor and environmental standards, cutbacks in investor protections, and potentially strengthened currency provisions. A clear expression of interest by the United States would give all current and potential CPTPP members hope for a stronger, larger, higher-standards alternative to RCEP while demonstrating a commitment to U.S. economic leadership in Asia. The United States should also welcome China's joining CPTPP, provided China implements changes to ensure that its laws, regulations, and practices are consistent with CPTPP upon its entry.

Protect U.S. Security Interests in BRI Countries

The U.S. response to BRI should focus predominantly on mitigating its economic and environmental harms, maintaining U.S. competitiveness in important BRI markets, and minimizing China's ability to leverage its economic influence to extract political concessions that harm U.S. interests.

The U.S. response, however, also has to ensure BRI projects do not impede its ability to defend its allies or operate out of strategic ports during a crisis. The United States should clearly communicate to its allies the limits of what they can accept under BRI and, in contingency plans, assume China will attempt to disrupt critical infrastructure in BRI countries by applying political and economic leverage.

> Create mitigation plans for possible Chinese disruption of critical infrastructure in BRI countries during a conflict to ensure defense capabilities.

China's ability to shut down a BRI country's telecommunications infrastructure, power grid, or railroads during a conflict in which the United States needs to operate from that BRI country in order to defend an ally represents a more serious threat to the United States than China's ability to collect intelligence on U.S. military operations.

Therefore, when planning for any contingency that calls for the United States to operate out of a BRI country in which China has built its critical infrastructure, the Department of Defense should assume the United States will be operating in a degraded or compromised information environment.

The Defense Department should invest additional resources in creating redundancies for the U.S. military, including securing additional access agreements to offset the possibility of access loss. It should also invest in network resiliency, or the ability to withstand exploitation of any single node or transmission path to optimize security and continuity of operations. Proactive information-sharing protocols and host nation agreements should be in place to enhance operations and safeguard information in countries with Chinese built or sourced physical and digital infrastructure.

Train cyber diplomats who can work with host governments to reduce the national security vulnerabilities of potentially sensitive BRI projects.

By using Chinese companies and technologies to build out critical infrastructure, such as 5G networks, allied nations can leave themselves especially vulnerable to political and economic coercion and even make mutual defense more difficult down the road. In some cases, the United States could seek to prevent a deal from being struck at all; in others, it could seek to ensure that Chinese components are not used to build the backbone of a network.

To help BRI countries assess the security risk of digital projects, the United States should develop a coterie of Foreign Service officers with deep expertise in cybersecurity and create cyber officer positions in embassies around the world. Currently, the International Communications and Information Policy division of the Bureau of Economic and Business Affairs is tasked with promoting secure 5G networks and working with partners on internet governance, but that office is overtaxed.

The State Department should elevate cyber policy, creating a unified Bureau for Cyberspace and the Digital Economy with an assistant secretary. Congress has introduced the bipartisan Cyber Diplomacy Act, which proposes to do just this, and should move forward with passage of the bill.[382]

Finally, the United States should work with allies and partners that cannot ban Chinese components fully from their networks to assess their network security and minimize the potential for harm.[383]

> Invest in undersea cables and undersea cable security to prevent them from being damaged or tapped.

More than 97 percent of all intercontinental electronic communications are transmitted through undersea cables, enabling government communications, international trade, and financial transactions.[384] To this point, undersea cable networks have proven remarkably resilient, but the possibility remains that an adversary could attempt to secretly tap a cable during peacetime in order to gather intelligence or sever cables entirely during a conflict in an effort to cut off communications, impede military operations, and cripple global financial markets. If a country wanted to do this, it would likely target the last mile of the cable and its landing station, the most vulnerable parts.[385]

Although the United States has access to many undersea cables, providing it with much-needed redundancy, many BRI countries are far more vulnerable. Greece, a NATO ally, relies on only three undersea cables, all of which share Athens as their landing point, to carry all of its traffic.[386] With China controlling the nearby port of Piraeus, its ability to threaten those cable systems should be taken seriously.

Undersea cables play a critical role in facilitating transcontinental communications and the ability of the U.S. military to operate during a crisis, and China has an increasing presence in ports around the world that are located near cable terminuses. The United States should minimize the chances that China can compromise these cables:

- It should encourage countries it could have to operate from in the future to bolster the physical security of their cable systems by mandating that manholes be welded shut, surveillance cameras be installed, and routine cable protection patrols be carried out.

- These countries should also ensure that they are continuously monitoring data usage flowing through the cables so they can detect abnormal activity.

- The United States should offer training programs and liaison opportunities with the Department of Homeland Security to build the capacity of countries to increase the security of their undersea cable systems and detect attempted intrusions.

- DFC should redouble its efforts to back new telecommunications cables, building off its recent investment in a cable directly connecting the United States with Indonesia and Singapore.[387]

CONCLUSION

The Belt and Road Initiative, Xi Jinping's signature foreign policy undertaking, is being recalibrated for a post–COVID-19 world. The building of roads, railways, ports, and power plants is giving way to a BRI centered on technology—primarily telecommunications, connectivity, health care, and financial services. China will also have to contend with the debt and environmental burdens that have accompanied BRI's signature infrastructure projects.

Facing the economic, political, climate, security, and health risks posed by BRI requires the United States to put in place a strategy that draws on its strengths—its innovative companies, deep capital markets, world-class research and educational institutions, strong alliances and partnerships with other countries, and a tradition of leadership in international organizations—to offer an alternative where it can and to push back where it needs to.

Through BRI, China began addressing long-standing needs of people living in developing countries for power and transportation, filling a void created when the United States and many of its partners and allies refrained from similar investments.

Although the United States cannot—and should not—completely fill that gap, it should strategically respond to BRI by

- addressing economic risks through support for debt relief and a reinvigoration of U.S. commercial diplomacy;

- improving its own competitiveness, particularly in the technology sector;

- working with allies, partners, and international organizations to offer an alternative to BRI and to promote higher standards; and

- shoring up its defenses against potential disruption of infrastructure.

  The United States needs a smart, tailored response that recognizes BRI is here to stay, albeit in a different form.

ENDNOTES

1. "Assessing China's Digital Silk Road Initiative," Council on Foreign Relations, http://cfr.org/china-digital-silk-road.

2. Strobe Talbott, "A Farewell to Flashman: American Policy in the Caucasus and Central Asia," U.S. Department of State, July 21, 1997, http://1997-2001.state.gov/regions/nis/970721talbott.html; Condoleezza Rice, "Remarks at Eurasian National University," U.S. Department of State, October 13, 2005, http://2001-2009.state.gov/secretary/rm/2005/54913.htm; and Hillary Rodham Clinton, "Remarks on India and the United States: A Vision for the 21st Century," U.S. Department of State, July 20, 2011, http://2009-2017.state.gov/secretary/20092013clinton/rm/2011/07/168840.htm.

3. Xi Jinping, "Work Together to Build the Silk Road Economic Belt and the 21st Century Maritime Silk Road," Xinhua, May 14, 2017, http://xinhuanet.com/english/2017-05/14/c_136282982.htm; "One Belt, One Road" is the literal translation of the Chinese name for the initiative (一带一路). Although China initially translated the initiative into English as "One Belt, One Road," it shifted and began referring to it as the "Belt and Road Initiative" in English (while not changing the Chinese characters used). In making this change, China could have been attempting to recast Belt and Road as more of an open-ended undertaking rather than one with a singular geostrategic thrust. This report uses Belt and Road Initiative, or BRI, in keeping with the new official translation.

4. For example, in 1999 China introduced a "Go West" campaign, which sought to build oil and gas pipelines between Western China and Central Asia. Some of these projects, which predate BRI, have now been subsumed under the BRI brand.

5. For the purposes of this report, the following 139 countries are counted as participants in BRI: Afghanistan, Albania, Algeria, Angola, Antigua and Barbuda, Armenia, Austria, Azerbaijan, Bahrain, Bangladesh, Barbados, Belarus, Benin, Bolivia, Bosnia and Herzegovina, Brunei, Bulgaria, Burundi, Cambodia, Cameroon, Cape Verde, Chad, Chile, Comoros, Cook Islands, Costa Rica, Cote d'Ivoire, Croatia, Cuba, Cyprus, Czech Republic, Democratic Republic of Congo, Djibouti, Dominica, Dominican Republic, Ecuador, Egypt, El Salvador, Equatorial Guinea, Estonia, Ethiopia, Fiji, Gabon, Georgia, Ghana, Greece, Grenada, Guinea, Guyana, Hungary, Indonesia, Iran, Iraq, Italy, Jamaica, Kazakhstan, Kenya, Kiribati, Kuwait, Kyrgyzstan, Laos, Latvia, Lebanon, Lesotho, Liberia, Libya, Lithuania, Luxembourg, Madagascar, Malaysia,

Maldives, Mali, Malta, Mauritania, Micronesia, Moldova, Mongolia, Montenegro, Morocco, Mozambique, Myanmar, Namibia, Nepal, New Zealand, Niger, Nigeria, Niue, North Macedonia, Oman, Pakistan, Panama, Papua New Guinea, Peru, Philippines, Poland, Portugal, Qatar, South Korea, Republic of the Congo, Romania, Russia, Rwanda, Samoa, Saudi Arabia, Senegal, Serbia, Seychelles, Sierra Leone, Singapore, Slovakia, Slovenia, Solomon Islands, Somalia, South Africa, South Sudan, Sri Lanka, Sudan, Suriname, Tajikistan, Tanzania, Thailand, The Gambia, Timor-Leste, Togo, Tonga, Trinidad and Tobago, Tunisia, Turkey, Uganda, Ukraine, United Arab Emirates, Uruguay, Uzbekistan, Vanuatu, Venezuela, Vietnam, Yemen, Zambia, Zimbabwe. This list was compiled by China's Leading Small Group for the Construction of One Belt, One Road (国家推进 "一带一路" 建设工作领导小组办公室), http://yidaiyilu.gov.cn/xwzx/roll/77298.htm; see also Wang Yi, "The Belt and Road Initiative Becomes New Opportunity for China-Latin America Cooperation," Ministry of Foreign Affairs of the People's Republic of China, September 18, 2017, http://www.fmprc.gov.cn/mfa_eng/zxxx_662805/t1494844.shtml.

6. Xi, "Work Together to Build the Silk Road Economic Belt."

7. "Xi Pledges to Bring Benefits to People Through Belt and Road Initiative," Xinhua, August 28, 2018, http://xinhuanet.com/english/2018-08/28/c_137423397.htm.

8. Tom Mitchell, "Beijing Insists BRI Is No Marshall Plan," *Financial Times*, September 25, 2018, http://ft.com/content/48f21df8-9c9b-11e8-88de-49c908b1f264.

9. Xi, "Work Together to Build the Silk Road Economic Belt"; Reuters, "China President Xi Says Goal of Belt and Road Is Advance 'Win-Win Cooperation,'" April 25, 2019, http://reuters.com/article/china-silkroad-xi/china-president-xi-says-goal-of-belt-and-road-is-advance-win-win-cooperation-idINB9N21901J.

10. Benn Steil and Benjamin Della Rocca, "Chinese Debt Could Cause Emerging Markets to Implode," *Foreign Affairs*, April 27, 2020, http://foreignaffairs.com/articles/east-asia/2020-04-27/chinese-debt-could-cause-emerging-markets-implode.

11. Although there is some disagreement over exactly how much Chinese policy bank lending has slowed, there is no dispute that the cutbacks have been significant and only partially offset by a smaller increase in Chinese commercial bank lending. Matthew Mingey and Agatha Kratz, "China's Belt and Road: Down but Not Out," Rhodium Group, January 4, 2021, http://rhg.com/research/bri-down-out.

12. Agatha Kratz, Daniel Rosen, and Matthew Mingey, "Booster or Brake? COVID and the Belt and Road Initiative," Rhodium Group, April 15, 2020, http://rhg.com/research/booster-or-brake-covid-and-the-belt-and-road-initiative; Agatha Kratz, Allen Feng, and Logan Wright, "New Data on the 'Debt Trap' Question," Rhodium Group, April 29, 2019, http://rhg.com/research/new-data-on-the-debt-trap-question; and Cissy Zhou, "China Slimming Down Belt and Road Initiative as New Project Value Plunges in Last 18 Months, Report Shows," *South China Morning Post*, October 10, 2019, http://scmp.com/economy/global-economy/article/3032375/china-slimming-down-belt-and-road-initiative-new-project.

13. Ministry of Foreign Affairs of the People's Republic of China, "President Xi Jinping Delivers Important Speech and Proposes to Build a Silk Road Economic Belt with Central Asian Countries," press release, September 7, 2013, http://fmprc.gov.cn/mfa_eng/topics_665678/xjpfwzysiesgjtfhshzzfh_665686/t1076334.shtml.

14. World Bank, *Belt and Road Economics: Opportunities and Risks of Transport Corridors* (Washington, DC: World Bank, 2019), http://worldbank.org/en/topic/regional-integration/publication/belt-and-road-economics-opportunities-and-risks-of-transport-corridors.

15. Chris Heathcote, "Forecasting Infrastructure Investment Needs for 50 Countries, 7 Sectors Through 2040," *World Bank Blogs*, August 10, 2017, http://blogs.worldbank.org/ppps/forecasting-infrastructure-investment-needs-50-countries-7-sectors-through-2040.

16. World Bank, *Belt and Road Economics*; *Meeting Asia's Infrastructure Needs* (Asian Development Bank, 2017) 39–48, http://adb.org/publications/asia-infrastructure-needs; and Martin Raiser and Michele Ruta, "Managing the Risks of the Belt and Road," *East Asia & Pacific on the Rise* (blog), World Bank, June 20, 2019, https://blogs.worldbank.org/eastasiapacific/managing-the-risks-of-the-belt-and-road.

17. Daisy Margaret Jane Streatfeild, "More Than 230 Million Reasons to Invest in Sustainable Infrastructure," *Hablemos de Sostenibilidad Y Cambio Climático* (blog), Inter-American Development Bank, November 14, 2017, http://blogs.iadb.org/sostenibilidad/en/more-than-230-million-reasons-to-invest-in-sustainable-infrastructure-2.

18. Matthew P. Goodman, Daniel F. Runde, Jonathan E. Hillman, and Erol Yayboke, *The Higher Road: Forging a U.S. Strategy for the Global Infrastructure Challenge* (Center for Strategic and International Studies, April 23, 2019), http://csis.org/higherroad; and Richard Bluhm, Axel Dreher, Andreas Fuchs, Bradley Parks, Austin Strange, and Michael Tierney, "Connective Financing: Chinese Infrastructure Projects and the Diffusion of Economic Activity in Developing Countries," AidData Working Paper 64, 2018, http://aiddata.org/china-project-locations.

19. Thomas Hale, Chuyu Liu, and Johannes Urpelainen, *Belt and Road Decision-Making in China and Recipient Countries: How and to What Extent Does Sustainability Matter?* (ISEP, BSG, and ClimateWorks Foundation, April 2020), http://sais-isep.org/wp-content/uploads/2020/04/ISEP-BSG-BRI-Report-.pdf.

20. Lee Jones and Shahar Hameiri, *Debunking the Myth of 'Debt-Trap Diplomacy': How Recipient Countries Shape China's Belt and Road Initiative* (Chatham House, August 2020), 8–9, http://chathamhouse.org/sites/default/files/2020-08-25-debunking-myth-debt-trap-diplomacy-jones-hameiri.pdf.

21. Gustavo de L.T. Oliveira and Margaret Myers, "The Tenuous Co-Production of China's Belt and Road Initiative in Brazil and Latin America," *Journal of Contemporary China*, 2020, http://tandfonline.com/doi/epub/10.1080/10670564.2020.1827358.

22. An authoritative source estimated that there were more than three thousand BRI projects underway by late 2018. *People's Daily Overseas Edition*, "央企承建 "一带一路" 项目3116个" (State-Owned Enterprises are constructing 3,116 projects under One Belt, One Road), October 31, 2018, http://gov.cn/xinwen/2018-10/31/content_5336052.htm.

23. *The Belt and Road Is Overhyped, Commercially: Statement Before the Senate Subcommittee on International Trade, Customs, and Global Competitiveness*, 116th Cong. (June 12, 2019) (testimony of Derek Scissors, Resident Scholar, American Enterprise Institute), http://finance.senate.gov/imo/media/doc/Derek%20Scissors%20-%20BRI%20Testimony.pdf. A Malaysian minister flatly asked his Chinese counterpart which projects the Chinese considered to be BRI in Malaysia, but the Chinese official could not give a response. Jones and Hameiri, *Debunking the Myth of 'Debt-Trap Diplomacy.'*

24. Cecilia Joy-Pérez and Derek Scissors, *Be Wary of Spending on the Belt and Road* (American Enterprise Institute, November 2018), http://aei.org/wp-content/uploads/2018/11/Updated-BRI-Report.pdf.

25. Jack Nolan and Wendy Leutert, "Signing Up or Standing Aside: Disaggregating Participation in China's Belt and Road Initiative," Brookings Institution, October 2020, http://brookings.edu/articles/signing-up-or-standing-aside-disaggregating-participation-in-chinas-belt-and-road-initiative.

26. Kai Schultz, "Sri Lanka, Struggling With Debt, Hands a Major Port to China," *New York Times*, December 12, 2017, http://nytimes.com/2017/12/12/world/asia/sri-lanka-china-port.html.

27. For example, Admiral Philip S. Davidson, Commander of U.S. Indo-Pacific Command, called BRI "a stalking horse to advance Chinese security concerns." Philip S. Davidson, "Philip S. Davidson on the United States' Interests in the Indo-Pacific," Lowy Institute, February 13, 2020, http://lowyinstitute.org/news-and-media/multimedia/audio/philip-s-davidson-united-states-interests-indo-pacific. U.S. Secretary of State Michael Pompeo accused China of trying to purchase an "empire" and vowed "to oppose them at every turn." Michael R. Pompeo, "Interview with Hugh Hewitt of the Hugh Hewitt Show," U.S. Department of State, October 26, 2018, http://state.gov/interview-with-hugh-hewitt-of-the-hugh-hewitt-show.

28. Xi, "Work Together to Build the Silk Road Economic Belt"; Xi Jinping, "Working Together to Deliver a Brighter Future For Belt and Road Cooperation," Ministry of Foreign Affairs of the People's Republic of China, April 26, 2019, http://fmprc.gov.cn/mfa_eng/zxxx_662805/tl1658424.shtml.

29. For example, China already reportedly exfiltrated data from the headquarters of the African Union (AU), after building the computer infrastructure for the AU. Ben Blanchard, "African Union Says Has No Secret Dossiers After China Spying Report," Reuters, February 8, 2018, http://reuters.com/article/us-china-africanunion/african-union-says-has-no-secret-dossiers-after-china-spying-report-idUSKBN1FS19W.

30. *From Silk Road to Silicon Road* (Chartered Institute of Building, May 2019), http://www.ciob.org/sites/default/files/CIOB-Cebr%20report%20-%20From%20Silk%20Road%20to%20Silicon%20Road.pdf; and François de Soyres, Alen Mulabdic, Siobhan Murray, Nadia Rocha, and Michele Ruta, "How Much Will the Belt and Road Initiative Reduce Trade Costs?" World Bank Group Policy Research Working Paper 8614 (October 2018), http://documents1.worldbank.org/curated/en/592771539630482582/pdf/WPS8614.pdf.

31. Daniel Russel and Blake Berger, *Navigating the Belt and Road Initiative* (Asia Society Policy Institute, June 2019), http://asiasociety.org/sites/default/files/2019-06/Navigating%20the%20Belt%20and%20Road%20Initiative_2.pdf.

32. Stephen G. Cecchetti, M. S. Mohanty, and Fabrizio Zampolli, "The Real Effects of Debt," Bank for International Settlements (BIS) Working Paper No. 352 (September 2011), http://bis.org/publ/work352.htm.

33. Davide Furceri and Aleksandra Zdzienicka, "How Costly Are Debt Crises?," IMF Working Paper No. 11/280 (December 2011), http://imf.org/en/Publications/WP/Issues/2016/12/31/How-Costly-Are-Debt-Crises-25400.

34. Johnathan Hillman, "China's Belt and Road Initiative: Five Years Later: Statement Before the Economic and Security Review Commission," January 25, 2018, 3, http://uscc.gov/sites/default/files/Hillman_USCC%20Testimony_25Jan2018_FINAL.pdf.

35. "ENR 2020 Top 250 Global Contractors," Engineering News-Record, 2020, http://enr.com/toplists/2020-Top-250-Global-Contractors-Preview.

36. David M. Lampton, Selina Ho, and Cheng-Chwee Kuik, *Rivers of Iron: Railroads and Chinese Power in Southeast Asia* (University of California Press, 2020).

37. Lampton, Ho, and Kuik, *Rivers of Iron*; and Randall Phillips, "Creating Market and Cultivating Influence: Testimony Before the U.S.-China Economic and Security Review Commission," January 25, 2018, http://uscc.gov/sites/default/files/Phillips_USCC%20Testimony_17Jan2018.pdf.

38. Asli Demirgüç-Kunt, Leora Klapper, Dorothe Singer, Saniya Ansar, and Jake Hess, *The Global Findex Database* (World Bank, 2017), http://globalfindex.worldbank.org.

39. Paul Triolo, Kevin Allison, and Clarise Brown, *The Digital Silk Road: Expanding China's Digital Footprint* (Eurasia Group, April 2020), http://eurasiagroup.net/live-post/digital-silk-road-expanding-china-digital-footprint.

40. Jack O'Dwyer, "FinTech in China: Growth Drivers and Trends," 1421, February 20, 2020, http://1421.consulting/2020/02/fintech-in-china-growth-drivers-trends.

41. Triolo, Allison, and Brown, *The Digital Silk Road*.

42. Rita Liao, "Jack Ma's Fintech Giant Tops 1.3 Billion Users Globally," TechCrunch, July 15, 2020, http://techcrunch.com/2020/07/14/ant-alibaba-1-3-billion-users. In 2019, Ant Group processed $17 trillion of transactions in mainland China, and a further $90 billion overseas. Peter Guest, "How Ant Group Built a $200 Billion Financial Empire," Rest of World, September 8, 2020, http://restofworld.org/2020/ant-group-financial-empire.

43. Triolo, Allison, and Brown, *The Digital Silk Road*.

44. "Quantifying Alipay & WeChat Pay's Phenomenal Growth," *PaymentsJournal*, September 3, 2020, http://paymentsjournal.com/quantifying-alipay-wechat-pays-phenomenal-growth; and "Do Alipay and Tenpay Misuse Their Market Power?," *Economist*, August 6, 2020, http://economist.com/finance-and-economics/2020/08/06/do-alipay-and-tenpay-misuse-their-market-power.

45. Economist Intelligence Group on Behalf of HSBC, "BRI: Rising to the Fintech Challenge," HSBC, August 9, 2018, http://business.hsbc.com/belt-and-road/bri-rising-to-the-fintech-challenge.

46. Economist Intelligence Group on Behalf of HSBC, "BRI."

47. "China's National Blockchain Infrastructure Takes Shape," *Ledger Insights*, 2019, http://ledgerinsights.com/chinas-national-blockchain-infrastructure-bsn; and Yaya J. Fanusie, "Don't Sleep on China's New Blockchain Internet," November 10, 2020, http://lawfareblog.com/dont-sleep-chinas-new-blockchain-internet.

48. *Blockchain-Based Service Network Introductory White Paper* (BSN Development Association: September 2019), http://liandufin.top/incubator/file/Blockchain-based%20Service%20Network%20(BSN)%20Introductory%20White%20Paper.pdf.

49. Ting Peng, "China's Blockchain Service Network Integrates Three More Public Chains," *Cointelegraph*, September 16, 2020, http://cointelegraph.com/news/chinas-blockchain-service-network-integrates-three-more-public-chains.

50. Fanusie, "Don't Sleep on China's New Blockchain Internet."

51. BSN Development Association, *Blockchain-Based Service Network Introductory White Paper*.

52. Nadia Schadlow and Richard Kang, "Financial Technology Is China's Trojan Horse," *Foreign Affairs*, January 13, 2021, https://foreignaffairs.com/articles/china/2021-01-13/financial-technology-chinas-trojan-horse.

53. Rita Liao, "The Race to Be China's Top Fintech Platform: Ant Vs. Tencent," *TechCrunch*, November 9, 2020, http://techcrunch.com/2020/11/09/tencent-vs-alibaba-ant-fintech; and Matt Fulco, "Chinese Fintech Giants Expand Across the Belt and Road," *SupChina*, February 14, 2020, http://supchina.com/2020/02/14/chinese-fintech-giants-expand-across-the-belt-and-road.

54. Fanusie, "Don't Sleep on China's New Blockchain Internet."

55. Yaya J. Fanusie and Emily Jin, "China's Digital Currency: Adding Financial Data to Digital Authoritarianism," Center for a New American Security, January 26, 2021, http://cnas.org/publications/reports/chinas-digital-currency.

56. Jevans Nyabiage, "Chinese Lenders Turn Off the Taps on International Energy Projects As 'Debt Trap Diplomacy' Criticisms Mount," *South China Morning Post*, February 20, 2020, http://scmp.com/news/china/diplomacy/article/3051466/chinese-lenders-turn-taps-international-energy-projects-debt; Kratz, Rosen, and Mingey, "Booster or Brake?"; and Haibin Zhu, Karen Li, Katherine Lei, and Grace Ng, "A Stress Test for China's Overseas Lending," JPMorgan Global Economic Research Note, July 9, 2020.

57. John Hurley, Scott Morris, and Gailyn Portelance, *Examining the Debt Implications of the Belt and Road Initiative from a Policy Perspective*, CGD Policy Paper 121 (Washington, DC: Center for Global Development, March 2018), http://cgdev.org/sites/default/files/examining-debt-implications-belt-and-road-initiative-policy-perspective.pdf; Luca Bandiera and Vasileios Tsiropoulos, "A Framework to Assess Debt Sustainability and Fiscal Risks Under the Belt and Road Initiative," World Bank Policy Research Working Paper 8891, June 2019, http://elibrary.worldbank.org/doi/abs/10.1596/1813-9450-8891.

58. *BRI Connect: An Initiative in Numbers*, 3rd ed. (Refinitiv) http://refinitiv.com/content/dam/marketing/en_us/documents/reports/belt-and-road-initiative-in-numbers-issue-3.pdf.

59. Tom Mitchell and Alice Woodhouse, "Malaysia Renegotiated China-Backed Rail Project to Avoid $5bn Fee," *Financial Times*, April 15, 2019, http://ft.com/content/660ce336-5f38-11e9-b285-3acd5d43599e; and Kanupriya Kapoor and Aye Min Thant, "Exclusive: Myanmar Scales Back Chinese-Backed Port Project Due to Debt Fears – Official," Reuters, August 2, 2018, http://reuters.com/article/us-myanmar-china-port-exclusive/exclusive-myanmar-scales-back-chinese-backed-port-project-due-to-debt-fears-official-idUSKBN1KN106.

60. "Kyrgyzstan Cancels China Logistics Super-Hub Investment After At-Bashy Protests," *Silk Road Briefing*, February 28, 2020, http://silkroadbriefing.com/news/2020/02/28/kyrgyzstan-cancels-china-logistics-super-hub-investment-al-bashy-protests; Marwaan Macan-Markar, "Thai Belt and Road Project Bumps Into Finance and Liability Issues," *Nikkei Asian Review*, September 12, 2019, http://asia.nikkei.com/Spotlight/Belt-and-Road/Thai-Belt-and-Road-project-bumps-into-finance-and-liability-issues; and "Cautious EU Holds China's Europe Ambitions in Check," *Nikkei Asian Review*, July 28, 2019, http://asia.nikkei.com/Spotlight/Belt-and-Road/Cautious-EU-holds-China-s-Europe-ambitions-in-check.

61. "China Says One-Fifth of Belt and Road Projects 'Seriously Affected' by Pandemic," Reuters, June 18, 2020, http://reuters.com/article/us-health-coronavirus-china-silkroad/china-says-one-fifth-of-belt-and-road-projects-seriously-affected-by-pandemic-idUSKBN23Q0I1.

62. Dzulfiqar Fathur Rahman, "Jakarata-Bandung High-Speed Railway Project Delayed Amid Pandemic," *Jakarta Post*, April 15, 2020, http://thejakartapost.com/news/2020/04/15/jakarta-bandung-high-speed-railway-project-delayed-amid-pandemic.html.

63. Gabriel Wildau and Nan Ma, "In Charts: China's Belt and Road Initiative," *Financial Times*, May 10, 2017, http://ft.com/content/18db2e80-3571-11e7-bce4-9023f8c0fd2e; and Christine Zhang and Jeffrey Gutman, "Aid Procurement and the Development of Local Industry: A Question for Africa," Brookings Institution Global Economy and Development Working Paper 88, June 2015, http://brookings.edu/wp-content/uploads/2016/07/aid-procurement-africa-zhang-gutman.pdf.

64. Nikki Sun, "China Development Bank Commits $250bn to Belt and Road," *Nikkei Asian Review*, January 15, 2018, http://asia.nikkei.com/Economy/China-Development-Bank-commits-250bn-to-Belt-and-Road.

65. Hale, Liu, and Urpelainen, *Belt and Road Decision-Making in China and Recipient Countries*.

66. For example, between 2000 and 2014, U.S. official finance was $394.6 billion, of which $366.4 billion (or 93 percent) was official development assistance given on concessional terms. Over that same period, China's official finance was $354.3 billion, of which only $81.1 billion (or 23 percent) was official development assistance. "China's Global Development Footprint," AidData, accessed December 29, 2020, http://aiddata.org/china-official-finance; and Scott Morris, Brad Parks, and Alysha Gardner, *Chinese and World Bank Lending Terms: A Systematic Comparison Across 157 Countries and 15 Years*, CGD Policy Paper 170 (Center for Global Development: April 2, 2020), http://cgdev.org/publication/chinese-and-world-bank-lending-terms-systematic-comparison.

67. Veasna Kong, Steven G. Cochrane, Brendan Meighan, and Matthew Walsh, *The Belt and Road Initiative Six Years On* (Moody's Analytics, June 2019), http://moodysanalytics.com/-/media/article/2019/belt-and-road-initiative.pdf.

68. Bushra Bataineh, Michael Bennon, and Francis Fukuyama, "How the Belt and Road Gained Steam: The Causes and Implications of China's Rise in Global Infrastructure," Stanford Center on Development, Democracy, and the Rule of Law, May 2019, http://cddrl.fsi.stanford.edu/publication/how-belt-and-road-gained-steam-causes-and-implications-china%E2%80%99s-rise-global.

69. Russel and Berger, *Navigating the Belt and Road Initiative*.

70. Roland Rajah, Alexandre Dayant, and Jonathan Pryke, *Ocean of Debt? Belt and Road and Debt Diplomacy in the Pacific* (Lowy Institute, October 21, 2019), http://lowyinstitute.org/publications/ocean-debt-belt-and-road-and-debt-diplomacy-pacific; Deborah Brautigam, "A Critical Look at Chinese 'Debt-Trap Diplomacy': The Rise of a Meme," *Area Development and Policy 5* (2020), http://doi.org/10.1080/23792949.2019.1689828; and Agatha Kratz, Matthew Mingey, and Drew D'Alelio, *Seeking Relief: China's Overseas Debt After COVID-19* (Rhodium Group, October 8, 2020), http://rhg.com/wp-content/uploads/2020/10/RHG_SeekingRelief_8Oct2020_Final.pdf.

71. Meg Rithmire and Yihao Li, "Chinese Infrastructure Investment in Sri Lanka: A Pearl or a Teardrop on the Belt and Road?," Harvard Business School Case 718-046, January 2019, https://www.hbs.edu/faculty/Pages/item.aspx?num=55410; Jones and Hameiri, *Debunking the Myth of 'Debt-Trap Diplomacy'.*

72. Agatha Kratz, Allen Feng, and Logan Wright, "New Data on the Debt Trap Question," Rhodium Group, April 26, 2019, http://rhg.com/research/new-data-on-the-debt-trap-question.

73. Jones and Hameiri, *Debunking the Myth of 'Debt-Trap Diplomacy.'*

74. *World Economic Outlook Update* (International Monetary Fund, January 2021), http://imf.org/en/Publications/WEO/Issues/2021/01/26/2021-world-economic-outlook-update.

75. Antoinette Sayeh and Ralph Chami, "Lifelines in Danger," *Finance & Development* 57, no. 2 (June 2020), http://imf.org/external/pubs/ft/fandd/2020/06/COVID19-pandemic-impact-on-remittance-flows-sayeh.htm.

76. *The Evolution of Public Debt Vulnerabilities in Lower Income Economies*, Policy Paper No. 20/003 (International Monetary Fund, February 10, 2020), http://imf.org/en/Publications/Policy-Papers/Issues/2020/02/05/The-Evolution-of-Public-Debt-Vulnerabilities-In-Lower-Income-Economies-49018.

77. Marc Jones, "Coronavirus Pushes Global Credit Rating Downgrade Threat to Record High," Reuters, May 27, 2020, http://reuters.com/article/us-health-coronavirus-ratings-downgrades/coronavirus-pushes-global-credit-rating-downgrade-threat-to-record-high-idUSKBN2331HU.

78. Bank for International Settlements, "Credit to the Non-Financial Sector," updated December 7, 2020, http://bis.org/statistics/totcredit.htm?m=6%7C380%7C669.

79. Kristalina Georgieva, "Policy Action for a Healthy Global Economy," *IMFBlog* (blog), March 16, 2020, http://blogs.imf.org/2020/03/16/policy-action-for-a-healthy-global-economy.

80. "COVID-19 Financial Assistance and Debt Service Relief," International Monetary Fund, updated December 21, 2020, http://imf.org/en/Topics/imf-and-covid19/COVID-Lending-Tracker; and "The IMF's Response to COVID-19," International Monetary Fund, updated March 4, 2021, http://imf.org/en/About/FAQ/imf-response-to-covid-19#q1.1.

81. Stephanie Segal, "Tracking International Financial Institutions' COVID-19 Response," Center for Strategic and International Studies, July 21, 2020, http://csis.org/analysis/tracking-international-financial-institutions-covid-19-response.

82. Kristalina Georgieva, "Press Briefing by Kristalina Georgieva Following a Conference Call of the International Monetary and Financial Committee," International Monetary Fund, March 27, 2020, http://imf.org/en/News/Articles/2020/03/27/tr032720-transcript-press-briefing-kristalina-georgieva-following-imfc-conference-call.

83. Sébastien Thibault, "The Pandemic Is Hurting China's Belt and Road Initiative," *Economist*, June 4, 2020, http://economist.com/china/2020/06/04/the-pandemic-is-hurting-chinas-belt-and-road-initiative; "Vice Foreign Minister Ma Zhaoxu Briefs on China's Participation in International Cooperation in COVID-19 Response," Ministry of Foreign Affairs of the People's Republic of China, June 8, 2020, http://fmprc.gov.cn/mfa_eng/wjbxw/t1787197.shtml; and James Kynge and Sun Yu, "China Faces Wave of Calls for Debt Relief on 'Belt and Road' Projects," *Financial Times*, April 30, 2020, http://ft.com/content/5a3192be-27c6-4fe7-87e7-78d4158bd39b.

84. Aida Dzhumashova, "Exim Bank of China to Reschedule Debt of Kyrgyzstan," 24.kg News Agency, April 29, 2020, http://24.kg/english/151447_Exim_Bank_of_China_to_reschedule_debt_of_Kyrgyzstan_.

85. Maria Abi-Habib and Keith Bradsher, "Poor Countries Borrowed Billions From China. They Can't Pay It Back," *New York Times*, May 18, 2020, http://nytimes.com/2020/05/18/business/china-loans-coronavirus-belt-road.html; and Meera Srinivasan, "Sri Lanka in Talks to Secure $500 Mn in Chinese Loans," *Hindu*, October 12, 2020, http://thehindu.com/news/international/sri-lanka-in-talks-to-secure-500-mn-in-chinese-loans/article32837581.ece.

86. G20, "Operational Guidelines for Sustainable Financing," March 2017, http://bundesfinanzministerium.de/Content/EN/Standardartikel/Topics/world/G7-G20/G20-Documents/g20-operational-guidelines-for-sustainable-financing.pdf?__blob=publicationFile&v=1; "IMF Institute Training at China-IMF Capacity Development Center (CICDC), Beijing, China," International Monetary Fund, accessed December 29, 2020, http://imf.org/en/Capacity-Development/Training/ICDTC/Schedule/CT; "Welcome to CICDC," China-IMF Capacity Development Center, accessed December 29, 2020, http://imfcicdc.org/content/cicdc/en.html; Ministry of Finance of the People's Republic of China and Asian Development Bank et al., "Memorandum of Understanding on Collaboration on Matters to Establish the Multilateral Cooperation Center for Development Finance," March 25, 2019, http://aiib.org/en/about-aiib/who-we-are/partnership/_download/collaboration-on-matters.pdf; G20, "Principles for Quality Infrastructure Investment," June 2019, http://mof.go.jp/english/international_policy/convention/g20/annex6_1.pdf; and Frank Tang, "China Seeks to Allay Belt and Road 'Debt Trap' Concerns With Standard for Assessing Financial Risk," *South China Morning Post*, April 25, 2019, http://scmp.com/news/china/diplomacy/article/3007714/china-seeks-allay-belt-and-road-debt-trap-concerns-standard.

87. Anuj Chopra, "G20 Declares Framework to Deepen Debt Relief for Poor Nations," *Agence France-Presse*, November 13, 2020, http://barrons.com/news/g20-declares-framework-on-debt-relief-for-poor-nations-01605277203?tesla=y.

88. World Bank Group and IMF, "Joint Statement World Bank Group and IMF Call to Action on Debt of IDA Countries," International Monetary Fund Press Release No. 20/103, March 25, 2020, http://imf.org/en/News/Articles/2020/03/25/pr20103-joint-statement-world-bank-group-and-imf-call-to-action-on-debt-of-ida-countries.

89. G20, "Communiqué: Virtual Meeting of the G20 Finance Ministers and Central Bank Governors," April 15, 2020, http://g20.utoronto.ca/2020/2020-g20-finance-0415.html; G20, "Communiqué: Virtual Meeting of the G20 Finance Ministers and Central Bank Governors," July 18, 2020, http://g20.org/en/media/Documents/Final%20G20%20FMCBG%20Communiqu%C3%A9%20-%20July%202020.pdf; Andrea Shalal, "G7 Ministers Urge Full Implementation of G20 Debt Freeze: U.S. Treasury," Reuters, July 13, 2020, http://reuters.com/article/us-health-coronavirus-g7/g7-ministers-urge-full-implementation-of-g20-debt-freeze-u-s-treasury-idUSKCN24E1SX; Jeremy Mark, "Where Does China Really Stand on Debt Relief?" *New Atlanticist* (blog), Atlantic Council, June 8, 2020, http://atlanticcouncil.org/blogs/new-atlanticist/where-does-china-really-stand-on-debt-relief; Abi-Habib and Bradsher, "Poor Countries Borrowed Billions From China."; Steil and Della Rocca, "Chinese Debt Could Cause Emerging Markets to Implode"; and Kynge and Yu, "China Faces Wave of Calls for Debt Relief on 'Belt and Road' Projects."

90. Liangyu, "China's Exim Bank's B&R Loans Surpasses 1 Trln Yuan," XinhuaNet, April 21, 2019, http://xinhuanet.com/english/2019-04/21/c_137996270.htm; Jason Lee, "China Development Bank Provides Over $190 Billion for Belt and Road Projects," Reuters, March 26, 2019, http://reuters.com/article/us-china-finance-cdb-bri/china-development-bank-provides-over-190-billion-for-belt-and-road-projects-idUSKCN1R8095; and Camilla Hodgson, "China Strikes Debt Deals With Poor Nations Under G20 Scheme," *Financial Times*, August 30, 2020, http://ft.com/content/6900c595-151b-4cfd-90bb-0be9967b7999.

91. Kevin Acker, "What We Know About China's Approach to Debt Relief: Insights From Two Decades of China-Africa Debt Restructuring," *Panda Paw Dragon Claw* (blog), August 31, 2020, http://pandapawdragonclaw.blog/2020/08/31/what-we-know-about-chinas-approach-to-debt-relief-insights-from-two-decades-of-china-africa-debt-restructuring; and Bandiera and Tsiropoulos, "A Framework to Assess Debt Sustainability."

92. Deborah Brautigam, "Chinese Debt Relief: Fact and Fiction," *Diplomat*, April 15, 2020, http://thediplomat.com/2020/04/chinese-debt-relief-fact-and-fiction; Joe Bavier, "IMF Approves Congo Republic Bailout After China Debt Deal," Reuters, July 11, 2019, http://reuters.com/article/us-congorepublic-imf/imf-approves-congo-republic-bailout-after-china-debt-deal-idUSKCN1U62NR; and Kratz, Mingey, and D'Alelio, *Seeking Relief*.

93. Paul Bartlett, "China Offers Cash-Strapped Kyrgyzstan a Glimmer of Hope on Debt," *Nikkei Asian Review*, December 3, 2020, http://asia.nikkei.com/Politics/International-relations/China-offers-cash-strapped-Kyrgyzstan-a-glimmer-of-hope-on-debt.

94. Organization of Economic Cooperation and Development, *China's Belt and Road Initiative in the Global Trade, Investment and Finance Landscape* (OECD, 2018), 13, http://oecd.org/finance/Chinas-Belt-and-Road-Initiative-in-the-global-trade-investment-and-finance-landscape.pdf.

95. *The 13th Five-Year Plan for Economic and Social Development of the People's Republic of China (2016–2020)*, (Beijing, China: Central Compilation & Translation Press), http://en.ndrc.gov.cn/newsrelease_8232/201612/P020191101481868235378.pdf.

96. "RCEP Text and Associated Documents," Australian Government Department of Foreign Affairs and Trade, accessed December 29, 2020, http://dfat.gov.au/trade/agreements/not-yet-in-force/rcep/rcep-text-and-associated-documents.

97. Peter A. Petri and Michael Plummer, "A New Trade Agreement That Will Shape Global Economics and Politics," *Order From Chaos* (blog), Brookings Institution, November 16, 2020, http://brookings.edu/blog/order-from-chaos/2020/11/16/rcep-a-new-trade-agreement-that-will-shape-global-economics-and-politics.

98. Petri and Plummer, "A New Trade Agreement."

99. "China's Trade With BRI Countries Surges to $1.3 Trillion in 2019," *Economic Times*, January 15, 2020, http://economictimes.indiatimes.com/news/international/business/chinas-trade-with-bri-countries-surges-to-1-34-trillion-in-2019/articleshow/73271222.cms.

100. David F. Gordon, Haoyu Tong, and Tabatha Anderson, *Beyond the Myths – Towards a Realistic Assessment of China's Belt and Road Initiative: The Development-Finance Dimension* (International Institute for Strategic Studies, March 2020) 16–17, http://iiss.org/blogs/research-paper/2020/03/beyond-the-myths-of-the-bri/.

101. Kratz, Rosen, and Mingey, "Booster or Brake?."

102. Zhu, Li, Lei, and Ng, "A Stress Test for China's Overseas Lending."

103. Faseeh Mangi, "China's Belt and Road Awakens With a Push Through Pakistan," Bloomberg, July 21, 2020, http://bloomberg.com/news/newsletters/2020-07-21/supply-chains-latest-pakistan-helps-revive-china-s-belt-and-road.

104. Adnan Aamir, "China-Iran Deal Overshadows Pakistan Belt and Road Project," *Nikkei Asian Review*, July 21, 2020, http://asia.nikkei.com/Spotlight/Belt-and-Road/China-Iran-deal-overshadows-Pakistan-Belt-and-Road-project; Farnaz Fassihi and Steven Lee Myers, "Defying U.S., China and Iran Near Trade and Military Partnership," *New York Times*, July 11, 2020, http://nytimes.com/2020/07/11/world/asia/china-iran-trade-military-deal.html.

105. Jude Blanchette and Jonathan Hillman, "China's Digital Silk Road After the Coronavirus," *Over the Horizon* (blog), Center for Strategic and International Studies, April 13, 2020, http://csis.org/analysis/chinas-digital-silk-road-after-coronavirus.

106. "State Councilor and Foreign Minister Wang Yi Chairs the High-Level Video Conference on Belt and Road International Cooperation," Ministry of Foreign Affairs of the People's Republic of China, June 19, 2020, http://fmprc.gov.cn/mfa_eng/zxxx_662805/t1790439.shtml; "Foreign Ministry Spokesperson Hua Chunying's Regular Press Conference on July 17, 2020," Ministry of Foreign Affairs of the People's Republic of China, July 18, 2020, http://fmprc.gov.cn/mfa_eng/xwfw_665399/s2510_665401/t1798656.shtml.

107. "Wang Yi Attends the Meeting of the Advisory Council of the Belt and Road Forum for International Cooperation," Ministry of Foreign Affairs of the People's Republic of China, December 19, 2020, http://fmprc.gov.cn/mfa_eng/zxxx_662805/t1841816.shtml.

108. Davide Strusani and Georges V. Houngbnon, *What COVID-19 Means for Digital Infrastructure in Emerging Markets* (International Finance Corporation, May 2020), http://ifc.org/wps/wcm/connect/publications_ext_content/ifc_external_publication_site/publications_listing_page/what+covid+19+means+for+digital+infrastructure+in+emerging+markets.

109. George Parker, Nic Fildes, Helen Warrel, and Demetri Sevastopulo, "UK Orders Ban of New Huawei Equipment From End of Year," *Financial Times*, July 14, 2020, http://ft.com/content/997da795-e088-467e-aa54-74f76c321a75; Li Tao, "Japan Latest Country to Exclude Huawei, ZTE From 5G Roll-out Over Security Concerns," *South China Morning Post*, December 10, 2018, http://scmp.com/tech/tech-leaders-and-founders/article/2177194/japan-decides-exclude-huawei-zte-government; Momoko Kidera, "Huawei's Deep Roots Put Africa Beyond Reach of US Crackdown," *Nikkei Asian Review*, August 15, 2020, http://asia.nikkei.com/Spotlight/Huawei-crackdown/Huawei-s-deep-roots-put-Africa-beyond-reach-of-US-crackdown.

110. For a more detailed look at CPEC, see Jonathan E. Hillman, *The Emperor's New Road: China and the Project of the Century* (New Haven: Yale University Press, 2020), 125–149; Andrew S. Small, *The China-Pakistan Axis: Asia's New Geopolitics* (Oxford: Oxford University Press, 2020), 183–212.

111. Daniel Markey, "How the United States Should Deal With China in Pakistan," *Carnegie-Tsinghua Center for Global Policy*, April 8, 2020, http://carnegietsinghua.org/2020/04/08/how-united-states-should-deal-with-china-in-pakistan-pub-81456; "CPEC game changer for region: Nawaz Sharif," *Gulf News*, February 28, 2017, http://gulfnews.com/world/asia/pakistan/cpec-game-changer-for-region-nawaz-sharif-1.1986146.

112. Stephanie Findlay, Farhan Bokhari, and Sun Yu, "Pakistan Seeks Relief from China Over Belt and Road," *Financial Times*, June 25, 2020, http://ft.com/content/4af8101b-599c-407d-8850-3fd27cd9b31c; Jeremy Page and Saeed Shah, "China's Global Building Spree Runs Into Trouble in Pakistan," *Wall Street Journal*, July 22, 2018, http://wsj.com/articles/chinas-global-building-spree-runs-into-trouble-in-pakistan-1532280460.

113. Page and Shah, "China's Global Building Spree Runs Into Trouble in Pakistan"; Isaac B. Kardon, Conor M. Kennedy, and Peter A. Dutton, *China's Maritime Report No. 7: Gwadar: China's Potential Strategic Strongpoint in Pakistan* (U.S. Naval War College, 2020), http://digital-commons.usnwc.edu/cgi/viewcontent.cgi?article=1006&context=cmsi-maritime-reports.

114. Mohammad Zafar, "Sickening Violence: Gunmen Kill 10 Labourers Execution-style in Gwadar," *Express Tribune*, May 13, 2017, http://tribune.com.pk/story/1408777/several-casualties-feared-gwadar-firing; Saeed Shah and Eva Dou, "Militants Attack Chinese Consulate in Pakistan," *Wall Street Journal*, November 23, 2018; Farhan Bokhari and Christian Shepherd, "Eight Killed in Attack on Hotel in Southwestern Pakistan," *Financial Times*, May 12, 2019; Saeed Shah, "Gunmen Attack Pakistan Stock Exchange, Citing Its Link to China," *Wall Street Journal*, June 29, 2020.

115. The IMF noted, "Over the medium term, the current account deficit is expected to peak at 3.4 percent of GDP in 2019 as CPEC-related imports gather steam, and could subsequently moderate as exports recover, supported by the elimination of supply-side bottlenecks and the implementation of business climate reforms. Pakistan will face increasing government and CPEC-related external repayment obligations, and external financing needs are projected to increase to nearly $7\frac{1}{2}$ percent of GDP over the medium term, highlighting the need for macroeconomic and structural policies supporting competitiveness." *Pakistan: 2017 Article IV Consultation Staff Report* (IMF, July 2017), http://imf.org/en/Publications/CR/Issues/2017/07/13/Pakistan-2017-Article-IV-Consultation-Press-Release-Staff-Report-Informational-Annex-and-45078; *Pakistan: Request for an Extended Arrangement Under the Extended Fund Facility-Press Release; Staff Report; and Statement by the Executive Director of Pakistan*, Country Report No. 19/212 (IMF, July 8, 2019), http://imf.org/en/Publications/CR/Issues/2019/07/08/Pakistan-Request-for-an-Extended-Arrangement-Under-the-Extended-Fund-Facility-Press-Release-47092.

116. The United States initially signaled it might oppose an IMF bailout given Pakistan's extensive borrowing from China, with U.S. Secretary of State Michael Pompeo commenting, "There's no rationale for IMF tax dollars—and associated with that,

American dollars that are part of the IMF funding—for those to go to bail out Chinese bondholders or—or China itself." In the end, however, the United States acquiesced. Mike Pompeo, interview by Michelle Caruso-Cabrera, *CNBC*, July 30, 2018, http://cnbc.com/2018/07/30/cnbc-exclusive-cnbc-transcript-us-secretary-of-state-mike-pompeo-s.html.

117. International Monetary Fund, "Statement at the Conclusion of the IMF Mission to Pakistan," February 14, 2020, http://imf.org/en/News/Articles/2020/02/14/pr2051-pakistan-statement-at-the-conclusion-of-the-imf-mission; *World Economic Outlook Update* (IMF, June 2020), http://imf.org/en/Publications/WEO/Issues/2020/06/24/WEOUpdateJune2020; The IMF's baseline scenario in order for Pakistan's debt to be sustainable assumed GDP growth of over two percent in 2020 and steadily higher rates of growth over the following four years. *Pakistan: Request for an Extended Arrangement Under the Extended Fund Facility – Press Release; Staff Report; and Statement by the Executive Director for Pakistan*; *World Economic Outlook Update*, (IMF, January 2021), http://imf.org/en/Publications/WEO/Issues/2021/01/26/2021-world-economic-outlook-update.

118. Findlay, Bokhari, and Yu, "Pakistan Seeks Relief From China Over Belt and Road"; Adnan Aamir, "Pakistan Belt and Road Railway Hits Snag as China Nixes Low Rate," *Nikkei Asian Review*, October 27, 2020, http://asia.nikkei.com/Spotlight/Belt-and-Road/Pakistan-Belt-and-Road-railway-hits-snag-as-China-nixes-low-rate.

119. For an in-depth examination of the Gwadar port, see Kardon, Kennedy, and Dutton, *China's Maritime Report No. 7: Gwadar: China's Potential Strategic Strongpoint in Pakistan*.

120. Saeed Shah, "Pakistan to Strengthen Its Control Over a Disputed Part of Kashmir," *Wall Street Journal*, November 2, 2020, http://wsj.com/articles/pakistan-to-strengthen-its-control-over-a-disputed-part-of-kashmir-11604324701.

121. Arif Rafiq, "The Pakistan Army's Belt and Road Putsch," *Foreign Policy*, August 26, 2020, http://foreignpolicy.com/2020/08/26/the-pakistan-armys-belt-and-road-putsch; Andrew Small, "Returning to the Shadows: China, Pakistan, and the Fate of CPEC," German Marshall Fund of the United States, September 2020, 6.

122. For example, when asked about China's treatment of the Uyghurs during a 2019 conversation at CFR, Imran Khan stated, "We don't make public statements, because that's how China is… I would not publicly talk about it." "A Conversation With Prime Minister Imran Khan of Pakistan," interview by Richard N. Haass, Council on Foreign Relations, September 23, 2019, http://cfr.org/event/conversation-prime-minister-imran-khan-pakistan-0.

123. Corinne Abrams and Saeed Shah, "U.N. Designates Pakistani as Terrorist After China Acquiesces," *Wall Street Journal*, May 1, 2019, http://wsj.com/articles/u-n-sanctions-pakistani-who-india-accuses-of-terrorism-11556729520.

124. Demetri Sevastopulo, Jim Brunsden, Sam Fleming, and Michael Peel, "Biden Team Voices Concern Over EU-China Investment Deal," *Financial Times*, December 22, 2020, quoting incoming National Security Adviser Jake Sullivan that the new administration would "welcome early consultations with our European partners on our common concerns about China's economic practices," http://ft.com/content/2f0212ab-7e69-4de0-8870-89dd0d414306; "Europe's Contested Deal With China Sends

Warning to Joe Biden," *Bloomberg News*, January 6, 2021, http://bloomberg.com/news/articles/2021-01-08/europe-s-contested-deal-with-china-sends-warning-to-joe-biden.

125. Eric Reguly, "Europe Hands China a Symbolic and Strategic Victory as Beijing Cracks Down on Democracy," January 8, 2021, *Globe and Mail*, http://theglobeandmail.com/business/commentary/article-europe-hands-china-a-symbolic-and-strategic-victory-as-beijing-cracks; Theresa Fallon, "The Strategic Implications of the China-EU Investment Deal," *Diplomat*, January 4, 2021, http://thediplomat.com/2021/01/the-strategic-implications-of-the-china-eu-investment-deal. The CAI will require approval of the European Parliament, with some parliamentarians expressing concern in light of Beijing's mass arrest of pro-democracy politicians in Hong Kong on January 6, 2021. Stuart Lau, "Hong Kong Arrests Threaten Passage of EU-China Investment Deal, European Parliament Members Say," *South China Morning Post*, January 7, 2021, http://scmp.com/news/china/diplomacy/article/3116713/european-parliament-members-say-hong-kong-arrests-threaten.

126. "Joint Communique of the Leaders' Roundtable of the 2nd Belt and Road Forum for International Cooperation," Xinhua, April 27, 2019, http://xinhuanet.com/english/2019-04/27/c_138016073.htm.

127. Antonio Guterres, "Remarks at the Opening of the Belt and Road Forum," United Nations, May 14, 2017, http://un.org/sg/en/content/sg/speeches/2017-05-14/secretary-general%E2%80%99s-belt-and-road-forum-remarks.

128. Nadège Rolland, *China's Eurasian Century?* (Washington, DC: National Bureau of Asia Research, 2017), 91, http://nbr.org/publication/chinas-eurasian-century-political-and-strategic-implications-of-the-belt-and-road-initiative.

129. Tang Siew Mun, Hoang Thi Ha, Anuthida Saelaow Qian, Glenn Ong, and Pham Thi Phuong Thao, *The State of Southeast Asia: 2020 Survey Report* (ISEAS-Yusof Ishak Institute, January 16, 2020), http://iseas.edu.sg/wp-content/uploads/pdfs/TheStateofSEASurveyReport_2020.pdf.

130. Mun, Ha, Qian, Ong, and Thao, *The State of Southeast Asia*.

131. For FDI figures, see UN Conference on Trade and Development (UNCTAD), *World Investment Report 2020: International Production Beyond the Pandemic* (New York, NY: UN, 2020), http://unctad.org/system/files/official-document/wir2020_en.pdf.

132. Mogopodi Lekorwe, Anyway Chingwete, Mina Okuru, and Romaric Samson, *China's Growing Presence in Africa Wins Largely Positive Popular Reviews*, Dispatch No. 122 (Afrobarometer, October 24, 2016), http://afrobarometer.org/sites/default/files/publications/Dispatches/ab_r6_dispatchno122_perceptions_of_china_in_africa1.pdf.

133. Shihar Aneez, "China's 'Silk Road' Push Stirs Up Resentment and Protest in Sri Lanka," Reuters, February 1, 2017, http://reuters.com/article/us-sri-lanka-china-insight/chinas-silk-road-push-stirs-resentment-and-protest-in-sri-lanka-idUSKBN15G5UT; Sun Narin, "'Our Ancestors' Graves Have Been Drowned': Cambodian Dam Wipes Out Hill Tribe Way of Life," *VOA Khmer*, December 7, 2018, http://voacambodia.com/a/our-ancestors-graves-have-been-drowned-cambodian-dam-wipes-out-hill-tribe-way-of-life/4689817.html.

134. Mun, Ha, Qian, Ong, and Thao, *The State of Southeast Asia*.

135. Tom Wright and Bradley Hope, "WSJ Investigation: China Offered to Bail Out Troubled Malaysian Fund in Return for Deals," *Wall Street Journal*, January 7, 2019, http://wsj.com/articles/how-china-flexes-its-political-muscle-to-expand-power-overseas-11546890449.

136. Bradley Hope, Tom Wright, and Scott Patterson, "1MDB Fugitive Jho Low Harbored by China, Malaysia Says," *Wall Street Journal*, August 17, 2018, http://wsj.com/articles/malaysia-says-china-harbors-1mdb-fugitive-1534459559.

137. Elnura Alkanova, "Abuse of Power? On the Trail of China's Mystery Millions in Kyrgyzstan," *Open Democracy*, October 24, 2018, http://opendemocracy.net/en/odr/what-happened-at-bishkek-power-plant; Andrew Higgins, "A Power Plant Fiasco Highlights China's Growing Clout in Central Asia," *New York Times*, July 6, 2019, http://nytimes.com/2019/07/06/world/asia/china-russia-central-asia.html.

138. John Reed, "China and Myanmar Sign Off on Belt and Road Projects," *Financial Times*, January 18, 2020, http://ft.com/content/a5265114-39d1-11ea-a01a-bae547046735.

139. Maria Abi-Habib, "How China Got Sri Lanka to Cough Up a Port," *New York Times*, June 25, 2018, http://nytimes.com/2018/06/25/world/asia/china-sri-lanka-port.html.

140. Andrew Small, *Returning to the Shadows: China, Pakistan, and the Fate of CPEC* (German Marshall Fund of the United States, September 2020), http://gmfus.org/publications/returning-shadows-china-pakistan-and-fate-cpec.

141. Steven Feldstein, "When It Comes to Digital Authoritarianism, China Is a Challenge—But Not the Only Challenge," *War on the Rocks*, February 12, 2020, http://warontherocks.com/2020/02/when-it-comes-to-digital-authoritarianism-china-is-a-challenge-but-not-the-only-challenge.

142. John Hemmings, "Reconstructing Order: The Geopolitical Risks in China's Digital Silk Road," *Asia Policy* 15, no. 1 (January 2020), 7, http://nbr.org/publication/reconstructing-order-the-geopolitical-risks-in-chinas-digital-silk-road.

143. Steven Feldstein, "Testimony Before the U.S.-China Economic and Security Review Commission: Hearing on China's Strategic Aims in Africa," May 8, 2020, http://uscc.gov/sites/default/files/Feldstein_Testimony.pdf; and Liza Lin and Josh Chin, "U.S. Tech Companies Prop Up China's Vast Surveillance Network," *Wall Street Journal*, November 26, 2019, http://wsj.com/articles/u-s-tech-companies-prop-up-chinas-vast-surveillance-network-11574786846.

144. Steven Feldstein, *The Global Expansion of AI Surveillance* (Washington, DC: Carnegie Endowment for International Peace, September 2019), http://carnegieendowment.org/files/WP-Feldstein-AISurveillance_final1.pdf.

145. Jonathan E. Hillman and Maesea McCalpin, "Watching Huawei's 'Safe Cities,'" Center for Strategic and International Studies, November 4, 2019, http://csis.org/analysis/watching-huaweis-safe-cities.

146. Joe Parkinson, Nicholas Bariyo, and Josh Chin, "Huawei Technicians Helped African Governments Spy on Political Opponents," *Wall Street Journal*, August 15, 2019, http://wsj.com/articles/huawei-technicians-helped-african-governments-spy-on-political-opponents-11565793017; Sheridan Prasso, "China's Digital Silk Road Is Looking More Like an Iron Curtain," Bloomberg, January 10, 2019, http://bloomberg.com/news/features/2019-01-10/china-s-digital-silk-road-is-looking-more-like-an-iron-curtain.

147. Prasso, "China's Digital Silk Road Is Looking More Like an Iron Curtain."

148. Feldstein, "Testimony Before the U.S.-China Economic and Security Review Commission."

149. He Huifeng, "In a Remote Corner of China, Beijing Is Trying to Export Its Model by Training Foreign Officials the Chinese Way," *South China Morning Post*, July 14, 2018, http://scmp.com/news/china/economy/article/2155203/remote-corner-china-beijing-trying-export-its-model-training.

150. "Application Proof of Megvii Technology Limited," *HKEX News*, August 25, 2019, http://www1.hkexnews.hk/app/appyearlyindex.html?lang=en&board=mainBoard&year=2019.

151. "Kenya: Want Growth? Look East," *African Business Magazine*, December 18, 2011, http://africanbusinessmagazine.com/uncategorised/kenya-want-growth-look-east; and Teddy Ng, "Kenya Looks East to 'Sincere Friend' in China," *South China Morning Post*, August 19, 2013, http://scmp.com/news/china/article/1297869/facing-icc-trial-kenyan-president-uhuru-kenyatta-welcomed-china-visit.

152. Muhammad Sabil Farooq, Yuan Tongkai, Zhu Jiangang, and Nazia Feroze, "Kenya and the 21st Century Maritime Silk Road," *China Quarterly of International Strategic Studies* 4, no. 3 (2018), http://worldscientific.com/doi/pdf/10.1142/S2377740018500136.

153. "The Vision," Kenya Vision 2030, http://vision2030.go.ke; BBC, "Kenyan Capital Nairobi Gets New Train," BBC, November 13, 2012, http://bbc.com/news/world-africa-20310767.

154. BBC, "Kenyan Capital Nairobi Gets New Train," BBC, November 13, 2012, http://bbc.com/news/world-africa-20310767; Although SGR was initially conceived before BRI, work on the project began in earnest after BRI's launch, and SGR is now considered a flagship BRI project in Africa; *Global Construction Review*, "Kenya's Court of Appeals Finds SGR Contract With China Road and Bridge Corporation Was Illegal," *Global Construction Review*, June 29, 2020, http://globalconstructionreview.com/news/kenyas-court-appeals-finds-sgr-contract-china-brid; "Mombasa-Nairobi Standard Gauge Railway Project," RailwayTechnology, accessed December 31, 2020, http://railway-technology.com/projects/mombasa-nairobi-standard-gauge-railway-project.

155. Feldstein, "Testimony Before the U.S.-China Economic and Security Review Commission."

156. Deborah Brautigam, Jyhjong Hwang, Jordan Link, and Kevin Acker, "Chinese Loans to Africa Database," China Africa Research Initiative, Johns Hopkins University School of Advanced International Studies, accessed December 29, 2020, http://chinaafricaloandata.org.

157. BBC, "Kenya Opens Nairobi-Mombasa Madaraka Express Railway," BBC, May 31, 2017, http://bbc.com/news/world-africa-40092600; Jevans Nyabiage, "Contract for Kenya's China-Funded Railway Ruled 'Illegal,'" *South China Morning Post*, June 23, 2020, http://scmp.com/news/china/diplomacy/article/3090225/contract-kenyas-china-funded-railway-ruled-illegal; Uwe Wissenbach and Yuan Wang, "African Politics Meets Chinese Engineers: The Chinese-Built Standard Gauge Railway Project in Kenya and East Africa," China Africa Research Initiative Working Paper No. 13, June 2017, http://static1.squarespace.com/static/5652847de4b033f56d2bdc29/t/594d739f3e00bed374

82d4fe/1498248096443/SGR+v4.pdf; Duncan Miriri, "Kenya Opens $1.5 Billion Chinese-Built Railway Linking Rift Valley Town and Nairobi," Reuters, October 16, 2019, http://reuters.com/article/us-kenya-railway/kenya-opens-1-5-billion-chinese-built-railway-linking-rift-valley-town-and-nairobi-idUSKBN1WV0Z0; Sui-Lin Tan and Jevans Nyabiage, "Kenya Keen to Renegotiate Debt, Fees With China as Coronavirus Hits Unprofitable Mombasa-Naivasha Rail Line," *South China Morning Post*, October 3, 2020, http://scmp.com/economy/china-economy/article/3103710/kenya-keen-renegotiate-debt-fees-china-coronavirus-hits.

158. "8 Quick Facts About Kenya's Standard Guade Railway," Xinhua, May 31, 2017, http://xinhuanet.com//english/2017-05/31/c_136328584.htm; Wissenbach and Wang, "African Politics Meets Chinese Engineers"; Still, SGR has suffered from low freight uptake, in part because of a lack of "point-to-point mobility" for shipments; Elaine K. Dezenski, "Below the Belt and Road: Corruption and Illicit Dealings in China's Global Infrastructure," *Foundation for Defense of Democracies*, May 6, 2020, http://fdd.org/analysis/2020/05/04/below-the-belt-and-road; Mwamoyo Hamza, "New Railway Halves Travel Time from Nairobi to Mombasa," *VOA News*, May 31, 2017, http://voanews.com/africa/new-railway-halves-travel-time-nairobi-mombasa.

159. Eric Olander, "Kenya: China Faces a Critical Test in Train Debt," *Africa Report*, September 30, 2020, http://theafricareport.com/43367/kenya-china-faces-a-critical-test-in-train-debt; David Herbling and Dandan Li, "China's Built a Railroad to Nowhere in Kenya," Bloomberg, July 18, 2019, http://bloomberg.com/news/features/2019-07-19/china-s-belt-and-road-leaves-kenya-with-a-railroad-to-nowhere; Nyabiage, "Contract for Kenya's China-Funded Railway Ruled 'Illegal'"; Dezenski, "Below the Belt and Road"; "Kenya Hits at China's Debt-Trap Diplomacy," *Sentinel*, July 2, 2020, http://sentinelassam.com/business/kenya-hits-at-chinas-debt-trap-diplomacy-486236; George Omondi, "Mombasa Port at Risk as Audit Finds it was Used to Secure SGR Loan," *East African,* December 20, 2018, http://theeastafrican.co.ke/tea/business/mombasa-port-at-risk-as-audit-finds-it-was-used-to-secure-sgr-loan-1408886.

160. BBC, "Kenya Opens Nairobi-Mombasa Madaraka Express Railway"; Paul Nantulya, "Implications for Africa from China's One Belt One Road Strategy," *Africa Center for Strategic Studies*, March 22, 2019, http://africacenter.org/spotlight/implications-for-africa-china-one-belt-one-road-strategy; Jevans Nyabiage, "China Meets Resistance Over Kenya Coal Plant, in Test of Its Africa Ambitions," *South China Morning Post*, July 14, 2019, http://scmp.com/news/china/diplomacy/article/3018489/china-meets-resistance-over-kenya-coal-plant-test-its-african; Aisha Salaudeen, "Kenya Launches the Second Phase of Its Billion-Dollar Chinese Railway Project," CNN, October 16, 2019, http://cnn.com/2019/10/16/africa/kenya-launches-chinese-railway-line/index.html; Wissenbach and Wang, "African Politics Meets Chinese Engineers"; "Mombasa - Nairobi Standard Gauge Line Funding Agreed," *Railway Gazette*, May 14, 2014, http://railwaygazette.com/news/infrastructure/single-view/view/mombasa-nairobi-standard-gauge-line-funding-agreed.html; Tan and Nyabiage, "Kenya Keen to Renegotiate Debt, Fees With China as Coronavirus Hits Unprofitable Mombasa-Naivasha Rail Line."

161. Dezenski, "Below the Belt and Road"; Herbling and Li, "China's Built a Railroad to Nowhere in Kenya"; Nyabiage, "Contract for Kenya's China-Funded Railway Ruled 'Illegal.'

162. "Kenya Halts Lamu Coal Power Project at World Heritage Site," BBC, June 26, 2019, http://bbc.com/news/world-africa-48771519; Dana Ullman, "When Coal Comes to Paradise," *Foreign Policy*, June 9, 2019, http://foreignpolicy.com/2019/06/09/when-coal-came-to-paradise-china-coal-kenya-lamu-pollution-africa-chinese-industry-bri; Mohamed Athman, *Lamu Old Town under Increased Pressure from Proposed Mega Infrastructure Development* (Berlin: World Heritage Watch, 2020), http://world-heritage-watch.org/wp-content/uploads/2020/06/WHW-Report-2020.pdf.

163. "Kenya Halts Lamu Coal Power Project at World Heritage Site."

164. Drazen Jorgic, "Kenya Says Chinese Firm Wins First Tender for Lamu Port Project," Reuters, April 11, 2013, http://reuters.com/article/kenya-port-lamu/kenya-says-chinese-firm-wins-first-tender-for-lamu-port-project-idUSL5N0CX38D20130411.

165. Ullman, "When Coal Comes to Paradise."

166. "Corruption Perceptions Index," Transparency International, accessed December 29, 2020, http://transparency.org/en/cpi/2019/results/ken#details; In some instances, contracts that provide Chinese companies privileges like guaranteed payments or priority access to revenues have only come to light through leaks. Dezenski, "Below the Belt and Road"; Even using Mombasa port as collateral for SGR loans only emerged when a report leaked from the Auditor-General's office; Omondi, "Mombasa Port at Risk as Audit Finds It Was Used to Secure SGR Loan."

167. Dezenski, "Below the Belt and Road."

168. Wissenbach and Wang, "African Politics Meets Chinese Engineers."

169. Duncan Miriri, "Kenya Forcing Importers to Use Costly New Chinese Railway, Businessmen Say," Reuters, December 3, 2019, http://reuters.com/article/us-kenya-railways/kenya-forcing-importers-to-use-costly-new-chinese-railway-businessmen-say-idUSKBN1Y70LT.

170. International Development Association and International Monetary Fund, *Joint World Bank-IMF Debt Sustainability Analysis* (May 2020), http://documents1.worldbank.org/curated/en/796991589998832687/pdf/Kenya-Joint-World-Bank-IMF-Debt-Sustainability-Analysis.pdf.

171. Dezenski, "Below the Belt and Road"; The SGR alone represents nearly 12 percent of Kenya's foreign debt obligations. Tan and Nyabiage, "Kenya Keen to Renegotiate Debt, Fees With China as Coronavirus Hits Unprofitable Mombasa-Naivasha Rail Line"; "Kenya Hits at China's Debt-Trap Diplomacy."

172. Duncan Miriri, "Kenya Should Renegotiate Chinese Rail Loan, Parliamentary Panel Says," Reuters, September 24, 2020, http://uk.reuters.com/article/kenya-railway-china/kenya-should-renegotiate-chinese-rail-loan-parliamentary-panel-says-idUKL5N2GL3T7; Olander, "Kenya: China Faces a Critical Test in Train Debt."

173. As a result of President Trump's decision to pull all American forces out of Somalia by January 15 and reposition them to Kenya, the U.S. military presence in close proximity to BRI projects in Kenya will expand. Helene Cooper, "Trump Orders All American Troops Out of Somalia," *New York Times*, December 16, 2020, http://nytimes.com/2020/12/04/world/africa/trump-somalia-troop-withdrawal.html.

174. Manuel Mogato, Michael Martina, and Ben Blanchard, "ASEAN Deadlocked on South China Sea, Cambodia Blocks Statement," Reuters, July 25, 2016, http://reuters.com/article/us-southchinasea-ruling-asean-idUSKCN1050F6; Javier C. Hernandez, Owen Guo, and Ryan Mcmorrow, "South Korean Stores Feel China's Wrath as U.S. Missile System Is Deployed," *New York Times*, March 9, 2017, http://nytimes.com/2017/03/09/world/asia/china-lotte-thaad-south-korea.html; Roel Landingin, "Philippines vs China: Going Bananas," *Financial Times*, May 11, 2012, http://ft.com/content/7f801f57-b7fc-3a54-9634-56a15c41fd3e; Richard Milne, "Norway Sees Liu Xiaobo's Nobel Prize Hurt Salmon Exports to China," *Financial Times*, August 15, 2013, http://ft.com/content/ab456776-05b0-11e3-8ed5-00144feab7de; Daniel McLaughlin, "EU on Guard as China Builds Infrastructure and Influence," *Irish Times*, November 22, 2018, http://irishtimes.com/news/world/europe/eu-on-guard-as-china-builds-infrastructure-and-influence-1.3705904.

175. Ben Westcott, "Australia Angered China by Calling for a Coronavirus Investigation. Now Beijing Is Targeting Its Exports," CNN, May 27, 2020, http://cnn.com/2020/05/26/business/china-australia-coronavirus-trade-war-intl-hnk/index.html; Aaron Clark, Kevin Varley, and Rajesh Kumar Singh, "Stranded Coal Ships Caught in Crosshairs of China-Australia Spat," Bloomberg, November 12, 2020, http://bloomberg.com/news/articles/2020-11-12/stranded-coal-ships-caught-in-crosshairs-of-china-australia-spat?srnd=markets-vp&sref=6ZE6q2XR.

176. Xi Jinping, "Fostering a New Development Paradigm and Pursuing Mutual Benefit and Win-win Cooperation," Xinhua, November 19, 2020, http://xinhuanet.com/english/2020-11/19/c_139527192.htm; Xi Jinping, "Some Major Issues of the National Medium- and Long-term Economic and Social Development Strategy" (国家中长期经济社会发展战略若干重大问题), *Qiushi*, October 31, 2020, http://qstheory.cn/dukan/qs/2020-10/31/c_1126680390.htm.

177. Marleen Heuer, "China Increases Influence Over Tibetan Refugees in Nepal," Deutsche Welle, August 29, 2016, http://dw.com/en/china-increases-influence-over-tibetan-refugees-in-nepal/a-19511365.

178. Wright and Hope, "WSJ Investigation: China Offered to Bail Out Troubled Malaysian Fund in Return for Deals."

179. "A Conversation with Prime Minister Imran Khan of Pakistan," Council on Foreign Relations.

180. Jacob Markell, "Dispute Settlement on China's Terms: Beijing's New Belt and Road Courts," Merics, February 14, 2018, http://merics.org/en/analysis/dispute-settlement-chinas-terms-beijings-new-belt-and-road-courts; Jonathan Hillman and Matthew Goodman, "China's 'Belt and Road' Courts to Challenge Current US-Led Order," *Financial Times*, June 24, 2018, http://ft.com/content/b64d7f2e-8f4d-11e8-b639-7680cedcc421; and Nyshka Chandran, "China's Plans for Creating New International Courts Are Raising Fears of Bias," *CNBC*, February 1, 2018, http://cnbc.com/2018/02/01/china-to-create-international-courts-for-belt-and-road-disputes.html.

181. Markell, "Dispute Settlement on China's Terms."

182. Goodman, Runde, Hillman, and Yayboke, "The Higher Road."

183. A deliverable from China's Second BRI Forum states, "China will initiate the experience sharing program for Belt and Road partner countries, inviting 10,000 representatives to China from these countries in the next five years, including those from political parties, political organizations, think tanks and social organizations, as well as senior political figures and scholars"; "List of Deliverables of the Second Belt and Road Forum for International Cooperation," Ministry of Foreign Affairs of the People's Republic of China, April 27, 2019, http://fmprc.gov.cn/mfa_eng/zxxx_662805/t1658767.shtml.

184. Xi, "Work Together to Build the Silk Road Economic Belt."

185. Ehsan Masood, "How China Is Redrawing the Map of World Science," *Nature*, May 1, 2019, http://nature.com/immersive/d41586-019-01124-7/index.html.

186. Alliance of International Science Organizations, *ANSO Annual Report: 2019*, anso.org.cn/publications/reports/202004/P020200409818352155102.pdf.

187. Giovanna De Maio, *Playing with Fire: Italy, China, and Europe* (Brookings Institution, May 2020), http://brookings.edu/research/playing-with-fire.

188. Jonathan E. Hillman, *The Emperor's New Road: China and the Project of the Century* (New Haven: Yale University Press, 2020), 95.

189. Michael Peel, Tom Hancock, Valerie Hopkins, and Miles Johnson, "China Ramps Up Coronavirus Help to Europe," *Financial Times*, March 18, 2020, http://ft.com/content/186a9260-693a-11ea-800d-da70cff6e4d3.

190. Kyle Anderson and Logan Pauley, "The Old Silk Road to Rome Gets New Life," *Diplomat*, March 22, 2019, http://thediplomat.com/2019/03/the-old-silk-road-to-rome-gets-new-life.

191. "Italy Signs on for Chinese 'Belt and Road' Port Investments," *Maritime Executive*, March 21, 2019, http://maritime-executive.com/index.php/article/italy-signs-on-for-chinese-belt-and-road-port-investments; Francesca Ghiretti, "Demystifying China's Role in Italy's Port of Trieste," *Diplomat*, October 15, 2020, http://thediplomat.com/2020/10/demystifying-chinas-role-in-italys-port-of-trieste.

192. Andrew MacDowall, "China Looks to Europe—Through the Balkans," *Financial Times*, December 19, 2014, http://ft.com/content/3f35bd16-f347-3ecc-82c0-0bcc6b5cdd0c; "China-Europe Freight Trains Hit Record High in 2020," Xinhua, January 11, 2021, http://xinhuanet.com/english/2021-01/11/c_139657810.htm#:~:text=BEIJING%2C%20Jan.,Railway%20Group%20Co.%2C%20Ltd; Nicola Capuzzo and Milano Finanza, "Italy Jumps on the Chinese Freight Link Bandwagon," trans. Sam Morgan, Euractiv, June 9, 2017, http://euractiv.com/section/economy-jobs/news/italy-jumps-on-the-chinese-freight-link-bandwagon; Jonathan E. Hillman, "The Rise of China-Europe Railways," Center for Strategic and International Studies, March 6, 2018, http://csis.org/analysis/rise-china-europe-railways.

193. Erik Brattberg and Philippe Le Corre, "The EU and China in 2020: More Competition Ahead," Carnegie Endowment for International Peace, February 19, 2020, http://carnegieendowment.org/2020/02/19/eu-and-china-in-2020-more-competition-ahead-pub-81096; European Commission, *EU-China—A Strategic Outlook*, Joint Communication to the European Parliament, the European Council, and the Council (European Commission, March 12, 2019) http://ec.europa.eu/commission/sites/beta-political/files/communication-eu-china-a-strategic-outlook.pdf.

194. Council of the European Union, "Council Conclusions on the Significance of 5G to the European Economy and the Need to Mitigate Security Risks Linked to 5G," December 3, 2019, http://consilium.europa.eu/media/41595/st14517-en19.pdf; European Commission, "Foreign Investment Screening: New European Framework to Enter into Force in April 2019," March 5, 2019, http://ec.europa.eu/commission/presscorner/detail/en/IP_19_1532.

195. Giuseppe Fonte and Elvira Pollina, "Italy Vetoes 5G Deal Between Fastweb and China's Huawei: Sources," Reuters, October 23, 2020, http://reuters.com/article/us-huawei-italy-5g/italy-vetoes-5g-deal-between-fastweb-and-chinas-huawei-sources-idUSKBN2782A5.

196. Erica Downs, *The China-Pakistan Economic Corridor Power Projects: Insights into Environmental and Debt Sustainability* (Columbia University Center on Global Energy Policy, October 2019), http://energypolicy.columbia.edu/sites/default/files/pictures/China-Pakistan_CGEP_Report_100219-2.pdf.

197. Kelly Sims Gallagher, Rishikesh Bhandary, Easwaran Narassimhan, and Quy Tam Nguyen, "Banking on Coal? Drivers of Demand for Chinese Overseas Investments in Coal in Bangladesh, India, Indonesia and Vietnam," *Energy Research and Social Science* 71 (January 2021), http://sciencedirect.com/science/article/pii/S2214629620304023?via%3Dihub.

198. Gallagher, Bhandary, Narassimhan, and Nguyen, "Banking on Coal?."

199. Brad Plumer, "The U.S. Will Stop Financing Coal Plants Abroad. That's a Huge Shift.," *Washington Post*, June 27, 2013, http://washingtonpost.com/news/wonk/wp/2013/06/27/the-u-s-will-stop-subsidizing-coal-plants-overseas-is-the-world-bank-next; Jake Schmidt, "World Bank to Stop Funding Coal Projects," *NRDC*, July 18, 2013, http://nrdc.org/experts/jake-schmidt/world-bank-stop-funding-coal-projects.

200. Harry Pearl, "China Slow to Curb Coal Financing as Japan, South Korea 'Accept New Reality' on Phasing Out Fossil Fuels," *South China Morning Post*, August 15, 2020, http://scmp.com/economy/global-economy/article/3097259/china-slow-curb-coal-financing-japan-south-korea-accept-new.

201. Ren Peng, Liu Chang, and Zhang Liwen, *China's Involvement in Coal-Fired Power Projects Along the Belt and Road* (Global Environmental Institute, May 2017), http://geichina.org/_upload/file/report/China's_Involvement_in_Coal-fired_Power_Projects_OBOR_EN.pdf; Allison Kirsch et al., *Banking on Climate Change: Fossil Fuel Finance Report 2020* (Rainforest Action Network, BankTrack, Indigenous Environmental Network, Oil Change International, Reclaim Finance, and the Sierra Club, 2020), http://ran.org/wp-content/uploads/2020/03/Banking_on_Climate_Change__2020_vF.pdf.

202. "China's Global Energy Finance," Boston University Global Development Policy Center, accessed February 19, 2020, http://bu.edu/cgef/#/all/Country-EnergySource.

203. Lihuan Zhou, Sean Gilbert, Ye Wang, Miquel Munoz Cabre, and Kevin P. Gallagher, "Moving the Green Belt and Road Initiative: From Words to Actions," World Resources Institute and Boston University Global Development Policy Center, October 2018, http://wriorg.s3.amazonaws.com/s3fs-public/moving-green-belt-and-road-initiative-from-words-to-actions.pdf; Nakano, "Greening or Greenwashing the Belt and Road Initiative?"

204. Emran Hossain, "China Backs 50pc Bangladesh Coal-Fired Projects: Report," *New Age*, November 21, 2019, http://newagebd.net/article/91246/china-backs-50pc-bangladesh-coal-fired-projects-report.

205. Pippa Gallop, Ioana Ciuta, and Wawa Wang, *Chinese-Financed Coal Projects in Europe* (CEE Bankwatch Network, December 10, 2019), http://bankwatch.org/publication/chinese-financed-coal-projects-in-europe.

206. Jan Ellen Spiegel, "The Potential Climate Consequences of China's Belt and Road Initiative," Yale Climate Connections, February 17, 2020, http://yaleclimateconnections.org/2020/02/the-potential-climate-consequences-of-chinas-belt-and-roads-initiative.

207. Katrina Northrop, "Coal Pushers: With a Domestic Glut, China Is Bankrolling Coal Projects Abroad—Even as the Rest of the World Cuts Back and China Pledges to Go Carbon Neutral," *Wire China*, September 27, 2020, http://thewirechina.com/2020/09/27/coal-pushers.

208. International Energy Agency, *CO2 Emissions From Fuel Combustion 2019 Highlights* (Paris: November 2019); David Eckstein, Marie-Lena Hutfils, and Mark Winges, *Global Climate Risk Index 2019* (Berlin: Germanwatch, December 2018), http://germanwatch.org/sites/germanwatch.org/files/Global%20Climate%20Risk%20Index%202019_2.pdf.

209. Downs, *The China-Pakistan Economic Corridor Power Projects.*

210. Peter Erickson, "New Oil Investments Boost Carbon Lock-in," *Nature* 526, September 2015, http://nature.com/articles/526043c.

211. Rebecca Ray, Kevin P. Gallagher, William Kring, Joshua Pitts, and B. Alexander Simmons, "Geolocated Dataset of Chinese Overseas Development Finance," BU Global Development Policy Center, http://bu.edu/gdp/chinas-overseas-development-finance.

212. World Wildlife Fund, *The Belt and Road Initiative: WWF Recommendations and Spatial Analysis,"* (WWF, May 2017), http://awsassets.panda.org/downloads/the_belt_and_road_initiative___wwf_recommendations_and_spatial_analysis___may_2017.pdf.

213. Tom Fawthrop, "Leaked Report Warns Cambodia's Biggest Dam Could 'Literally Kill' Mekong River," *Guardian*, May 16, 2018, http://theguardian.com/environment/2018/may/16/leaked-report-warns-cambodias-biggest-dam-could-literally-kill-mekong-river.

214. Elizabeth Losos, Alexander Pfaff, Lydia Olander, Sara Mason, and Seth Morgan, "Reducing Environmental Risks from Belt and Road Initiative Investments in Transportation Infrastructure," World Bank Group, January 2019, http://documents1.worldbank.org/curated/en/700631548446492003/pdf/WPS8718.pdf.

215. Spiegel, "The Potential Climate Consequences of China's Belt and Road Initiative."

216. Losos, Pfaff, Olander, Mason, and Morgan, "Reducing Environmental Risks from Belt and Road Initiative Investments in Transportation Infrastructure."

217. "Belt and Road Initiative Could Threaten Native Biodiversity," *Asian Scientist*, January 31, 2019, http://asianscientist.com/2019/01/in-the-lab/china-belt-road-initiative-biodiversity-invasive-species.

218. Le Hong Hiep, "The BRI's Footprint in the Lower Mekong Region," *Rosa Luxemburg Stiftung*, December 15, 2020, http://rosalux.de/en/news/id/43417/the-bris-footprint-in-the-lower-mekong-region.

219. Brian Eyler and Courtney Weatherby, "Mekong Mainstream Dams," Stimson Center, June 23, 2020, http://stimson.org/2020/mekong-mainstream-dams.

220. Brian Eyler, Regan Kwan, and Courtney Weatherby, "How China Turned Off the Tap on the Mekong River," Stimson Center, April 13, 2020, http://stimson.org/2020/new-evidence-how-china-turned-off-the-mekong-tap; Alan Basist and Claude Williams, *Monitoring the Quantity of Water Flowing Through the Upper Mekong Basin Under Natural (Unimpeded) Condition* (Bangkok: Sustainable Infrastructure Partnership, April 10, 2020), http://pactworld.org/library/monitoring-quantity-water-flowing-through-upper-mekong-basin-under-natural-unimpeded.

221. Hannah Beech, "China Limited the Mekong's Flow. Other Countries Suffered a Drought.," *New York Times*, April 13, 2020, http://nytimes.com/2020/04/13/world/asia/china-mekong-drought.html.

222. Beech, "China Limited the Mekong's Flow."

223. Eyler and Weatherby, "Mekong Mainstream Dams."

224. Jason Tower and Jennifer Staats, "China's Belt and Road: Progress on 'Open, Green and Clean?'," United States Institute of Peace, April 29, 2020, http://usip.org/publications/2020/04/chinas-belt-and-road-progress-open-green-and-clean.

225. Tower and Staats, "China's Belt and Road."

226. Lachlan Carey and Sarah Ladislaw, *Chinese Multilateralism and the Promise of a Green Belt and Road* (Center for Strategic and International Studies: November 2019), http://csis-website-prod.s3.amazonaws.com/s3fs-public/publication/191105_ChineseMultilateralismand_GreenBRI_FINALpdf.pdf.

227. "Belt and Road Initiative International Green Development Coalition (BRIGC)," UN Environment Program, accessed December 29, 2020, http://unenvironment.org/regions/asia-and-pacific/regional-initiatives/belt-and-road-initiative-international-green.

228. Carey and Ladislaw, *Chinese Multilateralism and the Promise of a Green Belt and Road*.

229. *China's Maritime Ambitions, Before the House Foreign Affairs Committee Subcommittee on Asia, the Pacific, and Non-Proliferation*, 116th Cong. (June 30, 2019) (testimony of Oriana Skylar Mastro, Resident Scholar, American Enterprise Institute), http://foreignaffairs.house.gov/hearings?ID=B0858A43-A17C-4AE4-A63C-78DB91A3B664.

230. Ian Storey, "China's 'Malacca Dilemma,'" Jamestown Foundation, April 12, 2006, http://jamestown.org/program/chinas-malacca-dilemma.

231. State Council Information Office of the People's Republic of China, "China's National Defense in the New Era," Xinhua, July 2019, http://xinhuanet.com/english/2019-07/24/c_138253389.htm.

232. Conor Kennedy, "Strategic Strong Points and Chinese Naval Strategy," China Brief (19: 6), Jamestown Foundation, March 22, 2019, http://jamestown.org/program/strategic-strong-points-and-chinese-naval-strategy.

233. For a detailed analysis of China's base in Djibouti, see Peter A. Dutton, Isaac B. Kardon, and Conor M. Kennedy, "China Maritime Report No. 6: Djibouti: China's First Overseas Strategic Strongpoint," U.S. Naval War College, April 2020, http://digital-commons.usnwc.edu/cgi/viewcontent.cgi?article=1005&context=cmsi-maritime-reports; Lauren Blanchard and Sarah Collins, *China's Engagement in Djibouti* (Congressional Research Service, September 4, 2019), http://crsreports.congress.gov/product/pdf/IF/IF11304/3.

234. Jeremy Page, Gordon Lubold, and Rob Taylor, "Deal for Naval Outpost in Cambodia Furthers China's Quest for Military Network," *Wall Street Journal*, July 22, 2019, http://wsj.com/articles/secret-deal-for-chinese-naval-outpost-in-cambodia-raises-u-s-fears-of-beijings-ambitions-11563732482; Philip Heijmans, "China Signs Secret Deal for Naval Outpost in Cambodia, WSJ Says," Bloomberg, July 22, 2019, http://bloomberg.com/news/articles/2019-07-22/china-signs-secret-deal-for-naval-outpost-in-cambodia-wsj-says.

235. Office of the Secretary of Defense, *Annual Report to Congress: Military and Security Developments Involving the People's Republic of China* (Department of Defense, 2019), 11, http://media.defense.gov/2019/May/02/2002127082/-1/-1/1/2019_CHINA_MILITARY_POWER_REPORT.pdf; Devin Thorne and Ben Spevak, *Harbored Ambitions: How China's Port Investments Are Strategically Reshaping the Indo-Pacific* (C4ADS, 2017), 21–22, http://c4ads.org/reports.

236. Isaac Kardon, "China's Military Power Projection and U.S. National Interests: Testimony Before the U.S.-China Economic and Security Review Commission," February 20, 2020, http://uscc.gov/sites/default/files/Kardon_Written%20Testimony.pdf.

237. Abi-Habib, "How China Got Sri Lanka to Cough Up a Port."

238. Wang Ruiqi, Gu Yuyuan, and Li Zhiqiang, "Gangkou Wuliu Junmin Ronghe Tixi Goujian Yanjiu [Research on Building Civil-Military Integration Systems in Port Logistics]" *Tantao Yu Yanjiu* [Discussion and Research], no. 10: 105–7; Zhang Jing, Zhang Zhihui, Zhou Jiangshou, "Zhong Mei Gangkou Jianshe Guanche Guofang Yaoqiu Dui Biao Fenxi [Comparison Between China and America in Implementation of National Defense Requirements in Port Construction]," *Junshi Jiaotong Xueyuan Xuebao* [Journal of Military Transportation University] 21, no. 4, 32–36; "China Navy," *IHS Jane's Fighting Ships Online*, 2019.

239. For a detailed discussion of Gwadar's suitability to host PLAN vessels, its potential value as a military base, and the contingencies in which the PLAN could want to operate from the port, see Kardon, Kennedy, and Dutton, *China's Maritime Report No. 7: Gwadar: China's Potential Strategic Strongpoint in Pakistan.*

240. Kardon, "China's Military Power Projection and U.S. National Interests."

241. Jayadeva Ranade, "How Coronavirus Is Stalling China's Military Modernisation Plans," *Hindustan Times*, February 19, 2020, http://hindustantimes.com/analysis/how-coronavirus-is-stalling-china-s-military-modernisation-plans/story-k733Qeay8VioryGr8V0aNM.html.

242. Ranade, "How Coronavirus Is Stalling China's Military Modernisation Plans."

243. Will Mackenzie, "Commentary: It's the Logistics, China," *National Defense*, June 10, 2020, http://nationaldefensemagazine.org/articles/2020/6/10/its-the-logistics-china; Ronald O'Rourke, *China Naval Modernization: Implications for U.S. Navy Capabilities—Background and Issues for Congress* (Congressional Research Service, July 30, 2020), http://fas.org/sgp/crs/row/RL33153.pdf.

244. For example, the 2015 deal for operation of Israel's port in Haifa was struck directly between the Shanghai International Port Group and Israeli Ministry of Transport; Michael Wilner, "U.S. Navy May Stop Docking in Haifa After Chinese Take Over Port," *Jerusalem Post*, December 15, 2018, http://jpost.com/Israel-News/US-Navy-may-stop-docking-in-Haifa-after-Chinese-take-over-port-574414.

245. Johnathan Hillman, *Influence and Infrastructure: The Strategic Stakes of Foreign Projects* (Center for Strategic and International Studies, January 22, 2019), http://csis.org/analysis/influence-and-infrastructure-strategic-stakes-foreign-projects.

246. Public-Private Analytic Exchange Program, *Threats to Undersea Cable Communications* (Office of the Director of National Intelligence, September 28, 2017), http://dni.gov/files/PE/Documents/1---2017-AEP-Threats-to-Undersea-Cable-Communications.pdf.

247. Akane Okutsu, Cliff Venzon, and CK Tan, "China's Belt and Road Power Grids Keep Security Critics Awake," *Financial Times*, March 10, 2020, http://ft.com/content/f2b6e395-f1ee-4a6d-8839-009a35555b52.

248. Phillip Cornell, "Energy Governance and China's Bid for Global Grid Integration," *EnergySource* (blog), Atlantic Council, May 30, 2019, http://atlanticcouncil.org/blogs/energysource/energy-governance-and-china-s-bid-for-global-grid-integration.

249. Okutsu, Venzon, and Tan, "China's Belt and Road Power Grids Keep Security Critics Awake."

250. Thomas S. Eder and Jacob Mardell, "Powering the Belt and Road," Merics, June 27, 2019, http://merics.org/en/analysis/powering-belt-and-road.

251. Cornell, "Energy Governance and China's Bid for Global Grid Integration"; Fortune Global 500 rankings, 2020, http://fortune.com/global500.

252. Cornell, "Energy Governance and China's Bid for Global Grid Integration."

253. Cornell, "Energy Governance and China's Bid for Global Grid Integration."

254. Keith Zhai and Kay Johnson, "Exclusive: Taking Power—Chinese Firm to Run Laos Electric Grid Amid Default Warnings," Reuters, September 15, 2020, http://reuters.com/article/china-laos/exclusive-taking-power-chinese-firm-to-run-laos-electric-grid-amid-default-warnings-idUSL8N2FW068.

255. Gordon, Tong, and Anderson, *Beyond the Myths – Towards a Realistic Assessment of China's Belt and Road Initiative*; "Assessing China's Digital Silk Road Initiative:

A Transformative Approach to Technology Financing or a Danger to Freedoms?" Council on Foreign Relations, http://cfr.org/china-digital-silk-road.

256. Ministry of Industry and Information Technology of the People's Republic of China, "工业和信息化部关于工业通信业标准化工作服务于'一带一路'建设的实施意见" ("Implementation Opinions on Standardization Work in Industrial Sector and Communications Industry Serving Belt and Road Initiative"), November 5, 2018, http://gov.cn/zhengce/zhengceku/2018-12/31/content_5442657.htm.

257. Ellen Nakashima, "U.S. Pushes Hard for a Ban on Huawei in Europe, But the Firm's 5G Prices Are Nearly Irresistible," *Washington Post*, May 29, 2019, http://washingtonpost.com/world/national-security/for-huawei-the-5g-play-is-in-europe--and-the-us-is-pushing-hard-for-a-ban-there/2019/05/28/582a8ff6-78d4-11e9-b7ae-390de4259661_story.html.

258. Hong Shen, "Building a Digital Silk Road? Situating the Internet in China's Belt and Road Initiative," *International Journal of Communication* 12, 2687, http://ijoc.org/index.php/ijoc/article/view/8405; Mercator Institute for China Studies, "Networking the Belt and Road—The Future Is Digital," Merics, August 28, 2019, http://merics.org/en/bri-tracker/networking-the-belt-and-road; Melanie Hart and Jordan Link, "There Is a Solution to the Huawei Challenge," Center for American Progress, October 14, 2020, http://americanprogress.org/issues/security/reports/2020/10/14/491476/solution-huawei-challenge.

259. Andrew Kitson and Kenny Liew, "China Doubles Down on Its Digital Silk Road," Reconnecting Asia, Center for Strategic and International Studies, November 14, 2019, http://reconnectingasia.csis.org/analysis/entries/china-doubles-down-its-digital-silk-road; Don Weinland, "China State Banks Pull Back from Risky Overseas Projects," *Financial Times*, April 4, 2019, http://ft.com/content/273c324c-55ec-11e9-a3db-1fe89bedc16e.

260. Sabrina Snell, *China's Development Finance: Outbound, Inbound, and Future Trends in Financial Statecraft* (U.S.-China Economic and Security Review Commission, December 16, 2015), http://uscc.gov/sites/default/files/Research/China%E2%80%99s%20Development%20Finance.pdf; Chuin-Wei Yap, "State Support Helped Fuel Huawei's Global Rise," *Wall Street Journal*, December 25, 2019, http://wsj.com/articles/state-support-helped-fuel-huaweis-global-rise-11577280736.

261. Lei Yu, Kimmo Sujopelto, Jukka Hallikas, and Ou Tang, "Chinese ICT Industry From Supply Chain Perspective—A Case Study of the Major Chinese ICT Players," *International Journal of Production Economics* 115 (October 2008), 374–387, http://sciencedirect.com/science/article/abs/pii/S0925527308001941?via%3Dihub.

262. Paul Triolo, Kevin Allison, Clarise Brown, and Kelsey Broderick, *The Digital Silk Road: Expanding China's Digital Footprint* (Eurasia Group, April 8, 2020), http://eurasiagroup.net/files/upload/Digital-Silk-Road-Expanding-China-Digital-Footprint-1.pdf.

263. This phenomenon takes place in the aircraft industry, where Boeing and Airbus are able to maintain dominant market positions in part because of their control over aftermarket services and upgrades. See Chris Isidore, "Boeing and Airbus Made Huge Mistakes, But Their Dominance Is Under No Threat," CNN, June 25, 2019, http://cnn.com/2019/06/25/business/boeing-airbus-duopoly/index.html.

264. Ma Si, "Huawei Secures Most 5G Contracts Around World," *China Daily*, February 22, 2020, http://global.chinadaily.com.cn/a/202002/22/WS5e50491ea3101282172796b9.html.

265. Amy Mackinnon, "For Africa, Chinese-Built Internet Is Better Than No Internet at All," *Foreign Policy*, March 19, 2019, http://foreignpolicy.com/2019/03/19/for-africa-chinese-built-internet-is-better-than-no-internet-at-all.

266. Louise Lucas, "Huawei Revenue Rises 39% Despite US Pressure on 5G," *Financial Times*, April 22, 2019, http://ft.com/content/2cdd5dec-64b6-11e9-9adc-98bf1d35a056.

267. Stefan Pongratz, "The Telecom Equipment Market 2019," Dell'Oro Group, March 2, 2020, http://delloro.com/the-telecom-equipment-market-2019.

268. 汪巍，"数字丝绸之路建设助力经济发展," 中国一带一路网 [Wang Wei, "The Construction of the Digital Silk Road Boosts Economic Development," *One Belt, One Road Portal*], November 25, 2017, http://yidaiyilu.gov.cn/ghsl/gnzjgd/36420.htm.

269. National Intelligence Law of the People's Republic, Chinese National People's Congress Network, adopted June 27, 2017, http://cs.brown.edu/courses/csci1800/sources/2017_PRC_NationalIntelligenceLaw.pdf.

270. Hong Shen, "Building a Digital Silk Road?," 2690.

271. Barry Noughton, "Chinese Industrial Policy and the Digital Silk Road: The Case of Alibaba in Malaysia," *Asia Policy* 15, no. 1 (January 2020), 23–39, http://nbr.org/publication/chinese-industrial-policy-and-the-digital-silk-road-the-case-of-alibaba-in-malaysia; Wong Ee Lin, "TNG Digital on the Road to Becoming Major e-Wallet Player," *Edge Financial Daily*, Edge Markets, July 29, 2019, http://theedgemarkets.com/article/tng-digital-road-becoming-major-ewallet-player.

272. 共建合作共赢之港——中国—东盟信息港平台作用日益凸显 ["Co-building a Win-win Port—China-ASEAN Information Port Platform Is Becoming Increasingly Prominent"], Xinhua, September 25, 2019, http://m.xinhuanet.com/2019-09/25/c_1125037543.htm.

273. Loni Prinsloo, "Huawei Strengthens Its Hold on Africa Despite U.S.-Led Boycott," Bloomberg, August 19, 2020, http://bloomberg.com/news/articles/2020-08-19/china-s-huawei-prospers-in-africa-even-as-europe-asia-join-trump-s-ban.

274. Hemmings, "Reconstructing Order."

275. "Smart Ports: Increasing Efficiency and Cutting Costs," ShipTechnology, June 19, 2018, http://ship-technology.com/features/smart-ports-increasing-efficiency-cutting-costs.

276. John Hemmings and Patrick Cha, "Exploring China's Orwellian Digital Silk Road," *National Interest*, January, 7, 2020, http://nationalinterest.org/feature/exploring-china's-orwellian-digital-silk-road-111731.

277. An example of this potential is China's alleged data extraction from the African Union headquarters. China built the Ethiopia-based headquarters, including its IT networks; Maylin Fidler, "African Union Bugged by China: Cyber Espionage as Evidence of Strategic Shifts," *Net Politics* (blog), Council on Foreign Relations, March 7, 2018, http://cfr.org/blog/african-union-bugged-china-cyber-espionage-evidence-strategic-shifts.

278. Henry Farrell and Abraham L. Newman, "Weaponized Interdependence: How Global Economic Networks Shape State Coercion," *International Security* 44, no. 1, 42–79, http://nsiteam.com/social/wp-content/uploads/2019/11/Farrell-and-Newman-2019-IS-Weaponised-interdependence.pdf.

279. Hilary McGeachy, "US-China Technology Competition: Impacting a Rules-Based Order," United States Studies Centre, May 2, 2019, http://ussc.edu.au/analysis/us-china-technology-competition-impacting-a-rules-based-order#china%E2%80%99s-approach-to-standards-setting.

280. On the BRI Action Plan of China's National Standards Committee, see 我国将推动5G、智慧城市等国标在"一带一路"沿线国家应用实施 [China Will Promote the Implementation of 5G, Smart City, and Other National Standards Along the Belt and Road]", Xinhua, December 22, 2017, http://xinhuanet.com/2017-12/22/c_1122155113.htm. On the promotion of technical standards by memoranda of understanding, see Adam Segal, "China's Alternative Cyber Governance Regime: Hearing Before the U.S.-China Economic Security Review Commission," March 13, 2020, http://uscc.gov/sites/default/files/testimonies/March%2013%20Hearing_Panel%203_Adam%20Segal%20CFR.pdf; Ray Bowen, "Beijing's Promotion of PRC Technical Standards: Written Testimony for the United States-China Economic and Security Review Commission," Pointe Bello, March 13, 2020, http://uscc.gov/sites/default/files/March%2013%20Hearing_Panel%203_Ray%20Bowen%20Pointe%20Bello%20v2.pdf.

281. Hart and Link, "There Is a Solution to the Huawei Challenge."

282. Hart and Link, "There Is a Solution to the Huawei Challenge."

283. Hideaki Ryugen and Hiroyuki Akiyama, "China Leads the Way on Global Standards for 5G and Beyond," *Nikkei Asian Review*, July 25, 2020, http://asia.nikkei.com/Politics/International-relations/China-leads-the-way-on-global-standards-for-5G-and-beyond; Edison Lee and Timothy Chau, *Telecom Services: The Geopolitics of 5G and IoT* (Jeffries, September 14, 2017), 27, http://jefferies.com/CMSFiles/Jefferies.com/files/Insights/TelecomServ.pdf.

284. Hart and Link, "There Is a Solution to the Huawei Challenge."

285. Alice Eckman, ed., Françoise Nicolas, Céline Pajob, John Seaman, Isabelle Saint-Mézard, Sophie Boisseau Du Rocher, and Tatiana Kastouéva-Jean, *China's Belt & Road and the World: Competing Forms of Globalization* (Paris: IFRI, April 2019), 35, http://ifri.org/sites/default/files/atoms/files/ekman_china_belt_road_world_2019.pdf.

286. Ngeow Chow-Bing, *COVID-19, Belt and Road Initiative, and the Health Silk Road* (Friedrich Ebert Stiftung, October 2020), http://library.fes.de/pdf-files/bueros/indonesien/16537.pdf.

287. An Baijie, "WHO, China Sign Pact Establishing 'Health Silk Road,'" *China Daily*, January 19, 2017, http://chinadaily.com.cn/business/2017wef/2017-01/19/content_27993857.htm.

288. State Council Information Office of the People's Republic of China, *White Paper: Fighting Covid-19: China in Action* (Beijing: State Council Information Office, June 7, 2020), Xinhua, http://xinhuanet.com/english/2020-06/07/c_139120424.htm.

289. Melanie Hart and Blaine Johnson, "Mapping China's Global Governance Ambitions," Center for American Progress, February 28, 2019, http://americanprogress.org/issues/security/reports/2019/02/28/466768/mapping-chinas-global-governance-ambitions.

290. Mercator Institute for China Studies, "China's 'Health Silk Road': Adapting the BRI to a Pandemic-Era World," Merics, November 25, 2020, http://merics.org/en/short-analysis/chinas-health-silk-road-adapting-bri-pandemic-era-world.

291. Kristine Lee and Martijn Rasser, "China's Health Silk Road Is a Dead-End Street," *Foreign Policy*, June 16, 2020, http://foreignpolicy.com/2020/06/16/china-health-propaganda-covid.

292. Lee and Rasser, "China's Health Silk Road Is a Dead-End Street."

293. Alberto Tagliapietra, "The European Union Won't Be Fooled by China's Health Silk Road," (blog), German Marshall Fund of the United States, September 2, 2020, http://gmfus.org/blog/2020/09/02/european-union-wont-be-fooled-chinas-health-silk-road.

294. For a more fulsome discussion of the global response to COVID-19 and lessons to be drawn from it, see CFR's Task Force report, *Improving Pandemic Preparedness: Lessons From COVID-19* (New York: Council on Foreign Relations, October 2020), http://cfr.org/report/pandemic-preparedness-lessons-COVID-19.

295. Gregory B. Poling and Kim Mai Tran, "America First Versus Wolf Warriors: Pandemic Diplomacy in Southeast Asia," Center for Strategic and International Studies, June 18, 2020, http://csis.org/analysis/america-first-versus-wolf-warriors-pandemic-diplomacy-southeast-asia.

296. "Factsheet: Jack Ma Foundation and Alibaba Foundation's Global Donations and Efforts to Combat COVID-19," *Alizila*, Alibaba Group, April 15, 2020, http://alizila.com/factsheet-jack-ma-foundation-alibaba-foundations-coronavirus-donations-and-efforts.

297. Kirk Lancaster, Michael Rubin, and Mira Rapp-Hooper, "Mapping China's Health Silk Road," *Asia Unbound* (blog), Council on Foreign Relations, April 10, 2020, http://cfr.org/blog/mapping-chinas-health-silk-road.

298. Deep Pal and Rahul Bhatia, "The BRI in Post-Coronavirus South Asia," Carnegie India, Carnegie Endowment for International Peace, May 26, 2020, http://carnegieindia.org/2020/05/26/bri-in-post-coronavirus-south-asia-pub-81814.

299. Mercator Institute for China Studies, "China's Vaccine Diplomacy Assumes Geopolitical Importance," Merics, November 24, 2020, http://merics.org/en/short-analysis/chinas-vaccine-diplomacy-assumes-geopolitical-importance.

300. Lancaster, Rubin, and Rapp-Hooper, "Mapping China's Health Silk Road."

301. Tagliapietra, "The European Union Won't Be Fooled by China's Health Silk Road."

302. Alice Su, "Faulty Masks. Flawed Tests. China's Quality Control Problem in Leading Global COVID-19 Fight," *Los Angeles Times*, October 4, 2020, http://latimes.com/world-nation/story/2020-04-10/china-beijing-supply-world-coronavirus-fight-quality-control; Pal and Bhatia, "The BRI in Post-Coronavirus South Asia."

303. Mercator Institute for China Studies, "China's 'Health Silk Road.'"

304. Keith Bradsher, "China Dominates Medical Supplies, in This Outbreak and the Next," *New York Times*, July 5, 2020, http://nytimes.com/2020/07/05/business/china-medical-supplies.html.

305. *2019 Report to Congress* (U.S.-China Economic and Security Review Commission, November 2019), http://uscc.gov/annual-report/2019-annual-report-congress; Chad P. Bown, "COVID-19: China's Exports of Medical Supplies Provide a Ray of Hope," *Trade and Investment Policy Watch* (blog), PIIE, March 26, 2020, http://piie.com/blogs/trade-and-investment-policy-watch/covid-19-chinas-exports-medical-supplies-provide-ray-hope.

306. "China Made 40 Face Masks for Every Person Around the World," Bloomberg News, January 14, 2021, http://bloomberg.com/news/articles/2021-01-14/china-made-40-face-masks-for-every-person-around-the-world.

307. *Safeguarding Pharmaceutical Supply Chains in a Global Economy, Before the House Committee on Energy and Commerce, Subcommittee on Health*, 116th Cong. (2019) (statement of Janet Woodcock, M.D., Director, Center for Drug Evaluation and Research), http://fda.gov/news-events/congressional-testimony/safeguarding-pharmaceutical-supply-chains-global-economy-10302019.

308. Pal and Bhatia, "The BRI in Post-Coronavirus South Asia."

309. *2019 Report to Congress.*

310. "Fact Sheet: The U.S. Government and Global Health," Kaiser Family Foundation, July 30, 2019, http://kff.org/global-health-policy/fact-sheet/the-u-s-government-and-global-health.

311. "Fact Sheet: The U.S. Government and Global Health."

312. Tiaji Salaam-Blyther, Luisa Blanchfield, Matthew C Weed, and Cory R. Gill, *U.S. Withdrawal from the World Health Organization: Process and Implications* (Congressional Research Service, October 21, 2020), http://fas.org/sgp/crs/row/R46575.pdf.

313. Chad P. Bown, "COVID-19: Trump's Curbs on Exports of Medical Gear Put Americans and Others at Risk," *Trade and Investment Policy Watch* (blog), PIIE, April 9, 2020, http://piie.com/blogs/trade-and-investment-policy-watch/covid-19-trumps-curbs-exports-medical-gear-put-americans-and.

314. Franco Ordoñez, "Trump Redirects Foreign Aid Agency to Work on Pandemic. Congress Has Questions," KPBS, July 17, 2020, http://kpbs.org/news/2020/jul/17/trump-redirects-foreign-aid-agency-to-work-on.

315. Eyck Freymann and Justin Stebbing, "China Is Winning the Vaccine Race: How Beijing Positioned Itself as the Savior of the Developing World," *Foreign Affairs*, November 5, 2020, http://foreignaffairs.com/articles/united-states/2020-11-05/china-winning-vaccine-race; "U.S.'s Azar Says Any U.S. Vaccine Would Be Shared Once U.S. Needs Met," Reuters, August 10, 2020, http://reuters.com/article/us-taiwan-usa-health-coronavirus-idUSKCN2560TV; Emily Rauhala, "Biden to Reengage With World Health Organization, Will Join Global Vaccine Effort," *Washington Post*, January 20, 2021, http://washingtonpost.com/world/biden-administration-who-covax/2021/01/20/3ddc25ce-5a8c-11eb-aaad-93988621dd28_story.html?tid=ss_tw.

316. Aarthi Swaminathan, "'Health Silk Road' Heats Up as China and U.S. Boost Efforts Amid Coronavirus," *Yahoo Finance*, May 11, 2020, http://finance.yahoo.com/news/health-silk-road-china-and-us-coronavirus-125036739.html?bcmt=1.

317. Sui-Lee Wee, "From Asia to Africa, China Promotes Its Vaccines to Win Friends," *New York Times*, September 11, 2020, http://nytimes.com/2020/09/11/business/china-vaccine-diplomacy.html.

318. Elizabeth Chen, "China's Vaccine Diplomacy Revamps the Health Silk Road Amid COVID-19," Jamestown Foundation, November 12, 2020, http://jamestown.org/program/chinas-vaccine-diplomacy-revamps-the-health-silk-road-amid-covid-19; Jacob Mardell, "China's Vaccine Diplomacy Assumes Geopolitical Importance," Merics, November 24, 2020, http://merics.org/en/short-analysis/chinas-vaccine-diplomacy-assumes-geopolitical-importance.

319. Jacob Mardell, "China's Vaccine Diplomacy Assumes Geopolitical Importance."

320. Jacob Mardell, "China's Vaccine Diplomacy Assumes Geopolitical Importance."

321. Raissa Robles, Alan Robles, and Bloomberg, "Duterte Seeks Chinese Coronavirus Vaccine, Rules Out US Bases in Philippines," *South China Morning Post*, July 27, 2020, http://scmp.com/week-asia/politics/article/3094918/duterte-seeks-chinese-coronavirus-vaccine-rules-out-us-bases.

322. Yanzhong Huang, "Why Mass Vaccination in the West Could Be Bad News for Chinese Leaders: To Narrow the Immunity Gap, China Could Be Forced to Prioritize its Domestic Vaccine Needs," *Think Global Health*, December 10, 2020, http://thinkglobalhealth.org/article/why-mass-vaccination-west-could-be-bad-news-chinese-leaders; Sui-Lee Wee, "China Wanted to Show Off Its Vaccines. It's Backfiring," *New York Times*, January 25, 2021, http://nytimes.com/2021/01/25/business/china-covid-19-vaccine-backlash.html.

323. For example, a $1.2 billion electricity project in Central Asia; Kevin Hartnett, "Should China's 'New Silk Road' Worry America?," *Politico*, May 26, 2015, http://politico.com/agenda/story/2015/05/china-america-silk-road-infrastructure-war-000031; USAID, "Power Africa: A 2017 Update," USAID Office of Press Relations, December 4, 2017, http://usaid.gov/news-information/press-releases/dec-4-2017-fact-sheet-power-africa-2017-update#:~:text=Launched%20in%20June%202013%2C%20Power,of%20 2015%2C%20to%20catalyze%20small.

324. More information on this initiative can be found at "Global Procurement Initiative," U.S. Trade and Development Agency, accessed December 31, 2020, http://ustda.gov/ustda-special-initiative/global-procurement-initiative.

325. In remarks in the Rose Garden with President Xi during a 2015 state visit, President Obama said of BRI and AIIB, "All of their aims are to expand mutual and beneficial cooperation with other countries and realize common development. These initiatives are open, transparent, inclusive. They are consistent in serving the interests of the U.S. and other countries' interest. And we will come—the U.S. and other parties—to actively participate in them." White House Office of the Press Secretary, "Remarks by President Obama and President Xi of the People's Republic of China in Joint Press Conference," White House Archives, September 25, 2016, http://obamawhitehouse.archives.gov/the-press-office/2015/09/25/remarks-president-obama-and-president-xi-peoples-republic-china-joint; Secretary of the Treasury Jacob Lew emphasized that it is "critical

that China be willing to embrace…high standards of governance and transparency in its own initiatives." Jacob J. Lew, "Prepared Remarks: Treasury Secretary Jacob J. Lew Remarks on U.S.-China Economic Relations at the American Enterprise Institute," AEI, June 16, 2016, http://aei.org/press/prepared-remarks-treasury-secretary-jacob-j-lew-remarks-on-u-s-china-economic-relations-at-the-american-enterprise-institute.

326. Gerald F. Seib, "Obama Presses Case for Asia Trade Deal, Warns Failure Would Benefit China," *Wall Street Journal*, April 27, 2015, http://wsj.com/articles/obama-presses-case-for-asia-trade-deal-warns-failure-would-benefit-china-1430160415.

327. Michael R. Pompeo, interview with Hugh Hewitt, *Hugh Hewitt Show*, October 26, 2018, http://state.gov/interview-with-hugh-hewitt-of-the-hugh-hewitt-show.

328. Mike Pence, "Prepared Remarks by Vice President Pence at 2018 APEC CEO Summit," White House, November 16, 2018, http://whitehouse.gov/briefings-statements/remarks-vice-president-pence-2018-apec-ceo-summit-port-moresby-papua-new-guinea.

329. John R. Bolton, "Remarks by National Security Advisor Ambassador John R. Bolton on the Trump Administration's New Africa Strategy," White House, December 13, 2018, http://whitehouse.gov/briefings-statements/remarks-national-security-advisor-ambassador-john-r-bolton-trump-administrations-new-africa-strategy.

330. Admiral Philip S. Davidson, "Philip S. Davidson on the United States' Interests in the Indo-Pacific," Lowy Institute, February 13, 2020, http://lowyinstitute.org/news-and-media/multimedia/audio/philip-s-davidson-united-states-interests-indo-pacific.

331. *Report to the U.S. Congress on Global Export Credit Competition* (EXIM, June 2020), http://exim.gov/sites/default/files/reports/competitiveness_reports/2019/EXIM_2019_CompetitivenessReport_FINAL.pdf.

332. EXIM's Charter states, "The Bank shall establish a Program on China and Transformational Exports to support the extension of loans, guarantees, and insurance, at rates and on terms and other conditions, to the extent practicable, that are fully competitive with rates, terms, and other conditions established by the People's Republic of China." *Export-Import Bank Act of 1945. Pub.* L. No. 116-94, 12 U.S.C. § 635 (2020), http://exim.gov/sites/default/files/exim-bank-2019-charter-as-amended.pdf; For more on the Program on China and Transformational Exports, see "Program on China and Transformational Exports," EXIM, accessed December 30, 2020, http://exim.gov/who-we-serve/external-engagement/program-on-china-and-transformational-exports.

333. "EXIM Board Unanimously Approves Historic Policy to Support U.S. Exporters Competing With the People's Republic of China," EXIM, December 18, 2020, http://exim.gov/news/exim-board-unanimously-approves-historic-policy-support-exporters-competing-peoples-republic.

334. Matthew Goodman, Daniel Runde, and Jonathan Hillman, "Connecting the Blue Dots," Center for Strategic and International Studies, February 26, 2020, http://csis.org/analysis/connecting-blue-dots.

335. The Blue Dot Network's webpage can be found at: "Blue Dot Network," U.S. Department of State, http://state.gov/blue-dot-network.

336. "Growth in the Americas: Frequently Asked Questions," U.S. Department of State, August 2019, http://state.gov/wp-content/uploads/2019/11/America-Crece-FAQs-003-508.pdf; Matt Youkee, "U.S. Makes Fresh Pitch to Latin America to Counter China's Influence," *Guardian*, October 1, 2020, http://theguardian.com/world/2020/oct/01/us-latin-america-china-beijing.

337. Department of Commerce Bureau of Industry and Security, "Addition of Entities to the Entities List," *Federal Register* 84, no. 98 (May 21, 2019), 22961, http://govinfo.gov/content/pkg/FR-2019-05-21/pdf/2019-10616.pdf.

338. Chris Miller, "America Is Going to Decapitate Huawei," *New York Times*, September 15, 2020, http://nytimes.com/2020/09/15/opinion/united-states-huawei.html.

339. Doina Chiacu and Stella Qiu, "Trump Says 'Dangerous' Huawei Could be Included in U.S.-China Trade Deal," Reuters, May 23, 2019, http://reuters.com/article/us-usa-trade-china/trump-says-dangerous-huawei-could-be-included-in-u-s-china-trade-deal-idUSKCN1ST0PA; Bob Davis, William Mauldin, and Lingling Wei, "Trump Allows U.S. Sales to Huawei as Trade Talks Resume," *Wall Street Journal*, June 29, 2019, http://wsj.com/articles/trump-says-he-is-set-to-discuss-huawei-with-xi-11561769726.

340. Roslyn Layton, "State Department's 5G Clean Network Club Gains Members Quickly," *Forbes*, September 4, 2020, http://forbes.com/sites/roslynlayton/2020/09/04/state-departments-5g-clean-network-club-gains-members-quickly/#12c2084c7536.

341. Michael R. Pompeo, "Secretary Michael R. Pompeo at a Press Availability," U.S. Department of State, August 5, 2020, http://state.gov/secretary-michael-r-pompeo-at-a-press-availability-10.

342. "Power Africa Fact Sheet," USAID, November 30, 2020, http://usaid.gov/sites/default/files/documents/power-africa-fact-sheet-11-2020.pdf.

343. "About CLDP," Commercial Law Development Program, Office of General Counsel, U.S. Department of Commerce, accessed December 30, 2020, http://cldp.doc.gov/about-cldp.

344. Paul Mozur and Raymond Zhong, "In About-Face on Trade, Trump Vows to Protect ZTE Jobs in China," *New York Times*, May 13, 2018, http://nytimes.com/2018/05/13/business/trump-vows-to-save-jobs-at-chinas-zte-lost-after-us-sanctions.html; Claire Ballentine, "U.S. Lifts Ban That Kept ZTE From Doing Business With American Suppliers," *New York Times*, July 13, 2018, http://nytimes.com/2018/07/13/business/zte-ban-trump.html.

345. Josh Lipsky and Jeremy Mark, "We Must Expand Debt Relief for Developing Countries," *Project Syndicate*, May 20, 2020, http://project-syndicate.org/commentary/covid19-developing-countries-need-more-debt-relief-by-josh-lipsky-and-jeremy-mark-2020-05.

346. *China's Foreign Aid (2014)* (Information Office of the State Council, July 2014), http://english.gov.cn/archive/white_paper/2014/08/23/content_281474982986592.htm.

347. World Bank Group, *International Debt Statistics 2020* (Washington, DC: World Bank, 2020), http://openknowledge.worldbank.org/bitstream/handle/10986/32382/9781464814617.pdf; Sebastian Horn, Carmen M. Reinhart, and Christoph Trebesch, "China's Overseas Lending," Working Paper 26050, NBER, July 2019, http://nber.org/system/files/working_papers/w26050/w26050.pdf.

348. Horn, Reinhart, and Trebesch, "China's Overseas Lending."

349. For example, such missions should not facilitate the export of coal power equipment. For examples of similar missions, see "Announcement of Upcoming May 2020 Through April 2021 International Trade Administration Missions," *Federal Register* 85 (May 2020), 12259–12267, http://federalregister.gov/documents/2020/03/02/2020-04210/announcement-of-upcoming-may-2020-through-april-2021-international-trade-administration-trade.

350. UN General Assembly, *Addis Ababa Action Agenda of the Third International Conference on Financing for Development (Addis Ababa Action Agenda)*, A/RES/69/313, August 17, 2015, http://undocs.org/A/RES/69/313.

351. Ben Kesling and Jon Emont, "U.S. Goes on the Offensive Against China's Empire-Building Funding Plan," *Wall Street Journal*, April 9, 2019, http://wsj.com/articles/u-s-goes-on-the-offensive-against-chinas-empire-building-megaplan-11554809402.

352. "Corrosive Capital," Center for International Private Enterprise, accessed December 30, 2020, http://corrosivecapital.cipe.org.

353. *FDI Qualities Indicators* (OECD, 2020), http://oecd.org/investment/FDI-Qualities-Indicators-Highlights.pdf.

354. Abigail Bellows, *Regaining U.S. Leadership on Anti-Corruption* (Carnegie Endowment for International Peace, July 1, 2020), http://carnegieendowment.org/2020/07/01/regaining-u.s.-global-leadership-on-anticorruption-pub-82170.

355. Helen Chen, "'Belt and Road' Projects Under Growing Scrutiny," (blog), Thompson Reuters, July 23, 2020, http://blogs.thomsonreuters.com/answerson/china-projects-fcpa.

356. Bellows, *Regaining U.S. Leadership on Anti-Corruption.*

357. *Innovation and National Security* (New York: Council on Foreign Relations, 2019), http://cfr.org/report/keeping-our-edge/pdf/TFR_Innovation_Strategy.pdf.

358. Milo Medin and Gilman Louie, *The 5G Ecosystem: Risks & Opportunities for DoD* (Defense Innovation Board, April 3, 2019), http://innovation.defense.gov/Portals/63/Templates/Updated%20Meeting%20Documents/5G%20UNCLASS%20PAPER_190404_FINAL.pdf.

359. Robert D. Atkinson, "Who Lost Lucent?: The Decline of America's Telecom Equipment Industry," *American Affairs Journal* 4, no. 3 (Fall 2020), http://americanaffairsjournal.org/2020/08/who-lost-lucent-the-decline-of-americas-telecom-equipment-industry/#notes; Medin and Louie, *The 5G Ecosystem.*

360. Eric Schmidt and Robert O. Work et al., *Interim Report and Third Quarter Recommendations* (National Security Commission on Artificial Intelligence, October 2020), http://nscai.gov/wp-content/uploads/2021/01/NSCAI-Interim-Report-and-Third-Quarter-Recommendations.pdf.

361. Medin and Louie, *The 5G Ecosystem*, 12.

362. *Innovation and National Security*, 19.

363. *The Importance of International Students to American Science and Engineering* (National Foundation for American Policy, October 2017), http://nfap.com/wp-content/uploads/2017/10/The-Importance-of-International-Students.NFAP-Policy-Brief.October-20171.pdf.

364. Will Hunt and Remco Zwetsloot, *The Chipmakers: U.S. Strengths and Priorities for the High-End Semiconductor Workforce* (Georgetown Center for Security and Emerging Technology, September 2020), http://cset.georgetown.edu/research/the-chipmakers-u-s-strengths-and-priorities-for-the-high-end-semiconductor-workforce.

365. Remco Zwetsloot, James Dunham, Zachary Arnold, and Tina Huang, *Keeping Top AI Talent in the United States* (Georgetown Center for Security and Emerging Technology, December 2019), http://cset.georgetown.edu/wp-content/uploads/Keeping-Top-AI-Talent-in-the-United-States.pdf.

366. Dennis Normille, "With Generous Funding and Top-Tier Jobs, China Seeks to Lure Science Talent From Abroad," *Science*, June 5, 2018, http://sciencemag.org/news/2018/06/generous-funding-and-top-tier-jobs-china-seeks-lure-science-talent-abroad.

367. Zwetsloot, Dunham, Arnold, and Huang, *Keeping Top AI Talent in the United States*.

368. Naomi Wilson, "Testimony Before the U.S.-China Economic and Security Review Commission," March 13, 2020, http://uscc.gov/sites/default/files/testimonies/March%2013%20Hearing_Panel%203_Naomi%20Wilson%20ITI.pdf.

369. Department of Commerce Bureau of Industry and Security, "Addition of Entities to the Entities List"; Bureau of Industry and Security, "Huawei Temporary General License Extension Frequently Asked Questions," BIS, May 18, 2020, http://bis.doc.gov/index.php/documents/pdfs/2446-huawei-entity-list-temporary-general-license-extension-faqs/file.

370. Wilson, "Testimony Before the U.S.-China Economic and Security Review Commission."

371. *2020 Annual Report to Congress* (U.S.-China Economic and Security Review Commission, December 2020), http://uscc.gov/annual-report/2020-annual-report-congress; *The China Challenge: Realignment of U.S. Economic Policies to Build Resiliency and Competitiveness, Before the U.S. Senate Committee on Commerce, Science, and Transportation, Subcommittee on Security*, 116th Cong. (2020) (statement of Dr. Rush Doshi, Director, Brookings Institution China Strategy Center), http://brookings.edu/wp-content/uploads/2020/08/Doshi-Commerce-Testimony-7.30.2020-Final.pdf.

372. Wilson, "Testimony Before the U.S.-China Economic and Security Review Commission."

373. The BUILD Act specifies, "The Corporation shall prioritize the provision of support under title II in less developed countries with a low-income economy or a lower-middle-income economy…The Corporation shall restrict the provision of support under title II in a less developed country with an upper-middle-income economy unless— (A) the President certifies to the appropriate congressional committees that such support

furthers the national economic or foreign policy interests of the United States; and (B) such support is designed to produce significant developmental outcomes or provide developmental benefits to the poorest population of that country." *Build Act of 2018*, H.R. 302, 115th Cong. (2018), http://dfc.gov/sites/default/files/2019-08/BILLS-115hr302_BUILDAct2018.pdf.

374. "About the Fund," TCX Fund, accessed December 31, 2020, http://tcxfund.com/about-the-fund.

375. Stu Woo, "U.S. to Offer Loans to Lure Developing Countries Away From Chinese Telecom Gear," *Wall Street Journal*, October 18, 2020, http://wsj.com/articles/u-s-to-offer-loans-to-lure-developing-countries-away-from-chinese-telecom-gear-11603036800?mod=hp_featst_pos3.

376. Aarthi Swaminathan, "U.S. Agency Created to Counter China's Soft Power Pledges $2 Billion to Renewable Energy Push," *Yahoo Finance*, December 21, 2020, http://uk.finance.yahoo.com/news/renweable-energy-dfc-usa-133140142.html.

377. "World Bank / IMF Spring Meetings 2018: Development Committee Communiqué," World Bank, April 21, 2018, http://worldbank.org/en/news/press-release/2018/04/21/world-bankimf-spring-meetings-2018-development-committee-communique.

378. Kate Hampton et al., *Green Development Guidance for BRI Projects Baseline Study Report* (Beijing: BRI International Green Development Coalition, December 2020), http://green-bri.org/green-bri-development-guidance-puts-coal-in-negative-list; "Convention on Environmental Impact Assessment in a Transboundary Context," opened for signature February 25, 1991, *United Nations Treaty Series* 1989, 309, http://treaties.un.org/Pages/ViewDetails.aspx?src=TREATY&mtdsg_no=XXVII-4&chapter=27&lang=en.

379. Lachlan Carey and Sarah Ladislaw, "Chinese Multilateralism and the Promise of a Green Belt and Road," Center for Strategic and International Studies, November 5, 2019, http://csis.org/analysis/chinese-multilateralism-and-promise-green-belt-and-road.

380. Carey and Ladislaw, "Chinese Multilateralism and the Promise of a Green Belt and Road,"; African Development Bank et al., *Climate Finance*, (AfDB, August 2019), http://eib.org/attachments/press/1257-joint-report-on-mdbs-climate-finance-2019.pdf.

381. Carey and Ladislaw, "Chinese Multilateralism and the Promise of a Green Belt and Road."

382. *Cyber Diplomacy Act of 2019*, H.R. 739, 116th Cong. (2019), http://congress.gov/bill/116th-congress/house-bill/739/text.

383. *Innovation and National Security*, 59.

384. Public-Private Analytic Exchange Program, *Threats to Undersea Cable Communications*.

385. Public-Private Analytic Exchange Program, *Threats to Undersea Cable Communications*, 7.

386. "Submarine Cable Map," TeleGeography, accessed December 30, 2020, http://submarinecablemap.com/#/landing-point/athens-greece.

387. Press Release, "DFC Approves Nearly $900 Million for Global Development Projects," U.S. Development Finance Corporation, March 12, 2020, http://dfc.gov/media/press-releases/dfc-approves-nearly-900-million-global-development-projects.

ACRONYMS

4G LTE
fourth-generation long-term
evolution

5G
fifth-generation

AI
artificial intelligence

AIIB
Asian Infrastructure
Investment Bank

ANSO
Alliance of International
Science Organizations

APEC
Asia-Pacific Economic
Cooperation

API
active pharmaceutical
ingredients

ASEAN
Association of Southeast
Asian Nations

BIT
bilateral investment treaty

BDN
Blue Dot Network

BRI
Belt and Road Initiative

BRIGC
BRI International Green
Development Coalition

BSN
Blockchain Service Network

BUILD Act
Better Utilization of Investments
Leading to Development Act

CAI
Comprehensive Agreement
on Investment

CAS
Chinese Academy of Sciences

CCP
Chinese Communist Party

CDB
China Development Bank

China EXIM
Export-Import Bank of China

CFR
Council on Foreign Relations

CLDP
Commercial Law and
Development Program

CPEC
China-Pakistan Economic
Corridor

CPTPP
Comprehensive and
Progressive Agreement for
Trans-Pacific Partnership

DFC
Development Finance
Corporation

DSR
Digital Silk Road

EU
European Union

FCPA
Foreign Corrupt Practices Act

FDI
foreign direct investment

fintech
financial services technology

FY
fiscal year

GDP
gross domestic product

GEIDCO
Global Energy Interconnection Development and Cooperation Organization

GIP
Green Investment Principles for Belt and Road Development

GPS
Global Positioning System

G7
Group of Seven

G20
Group of Twenty

HSR
Health Silk Road

ICT
information, communications, and technology

IDA
International Development Association

IEC
International Electrotechnical Commission

IFI
international financial institution

IMF
International Monetary Fund

ISO
International Organization for Standardization

ITU
International Telecommunications Union

LED
light-emitting diode

MDB
multilateral development bank

MFA
China's Ministry of Foreign Affairs

MOFCOM
China's Ministry of Commerce

MOU
memorandum of understanding

NATO
North Atlantic Treaty Organization

NDRC
China's National Development and Reform Commission

NGO
nongovernmental organization

NIST
National Institute of Standards and Technology

OECD
Organization for Economic Cooperation and Development

OPIC
Overseas Private Investment Corporation

PLA
People's Liberation Army

PLAN
People's Liberation Army Navy

PPE
personal protective equipment

RCEP
Regional Comprehensive Economic Partnership

R&D
research and development

SCS
South China Sea

SEZ
special economic zone

SGCC
State Grid Corporation of China

SGR
standard gauge railway

SMEs
small- and medium-sized enterprises

SOE
state-owned enterprise

STEM
science, technology, engineering, and mathematics

TAF
Transaction Advisory Fund

TCX
Currency Exchange Fund

THAAD
Terminal High Altitude Area Defense

TPP
Trans-Pacific Partnership

UNESCO
UN Educational, Scientific and Cultural Organization

USAID
U.S. Agency for International Development

USTDA
U.S. Trade and Development Agency

U.S. EXIM
Export-Import Bank of the United States

WHO
World Health Organization

WTO
World Trade Organization

1MDB
1Malaysia Development Berhad

TASK FORCE MEMBERS

Task Force members are asked to join a consensus signifying that they endorse "the general policy thrust and judgments reached by the group, though not necessarily every finding and recommendation." They participate in the Task Force in their individual, not institutional, capacities.

B. Marc Allen is a trustee of the Trilateral Commission, North American Group. He is chief strategy officer and senior vice president for strategy and corporate development of the Boeing Company. Allen was appointed to the Boeing Executive Council in 2014, reporting to the chairman. He has held a number of senior leadership positions, including president of Embraer partnership and group operations, president of Boeing International, president of Boeing Capital Corporation, vice president of Boeing International and president of Boeing China, and vice president for global law affairs and general counsel to Boeing International. Before Boeing, Allen practiced law in Washington, DC, served as U.S. Supreme Court Justice Anthony M. Kennedy's law clerk, and worked in strategy consulting and start-up leadership. Allen is an Aspen Institute Henry Crown fellow and sits on the boards of numerous global organizations. He received his bachelor's degree from Princeton University and his law degree from Yale Law School.

Charlene Barshefsky is senior international partner and international trade and investment group chair at WilmerHale in Washington, DC, where she advises multinationals and private equity firms on their global market access, investment, and acquisition strategies. She joined WilmerHale after serving in President Bill Clinton's cabinet as the U.S. trade representative (USTR) from 1997 to 2001 and previously as acting and deputy

USTR from 1993 to 1996. As the USTR, Barshefsky formulated U.S. trade policy and negotiated hundreds of complex trade and investment agreements that opened markets and removed regulatory and investment barriers worldwide. Barshefsky was the architect and negotiator of China's Word Trade Organization agreement, opening China's economy as a worldwide market. She negotiated landmark global agreements in financial services, telecommunications, technology products, and cyberspace, alongside comprehensive agreements with Jordan, Vietnam, and Latin America, among others. Barshefsky serves on the boards of the American Express Company, the Estee Lauder Companies, and MDC Partners. She is a trustee of the Howard Hughes Medical Institute and a nonresident senior fellow at Yale Law School's Paul Tsai China Center.

Brendan P. Bechtel is chairman and chief executive officer of Bechtel Group, Inc. He has held roles of increasing responsibility in field construction, project management, and executive leadership. He served as president and chief operating officer from 2014 to 2016, was named chief executive officer in 2016, and was elected chairman in 2017. Bechtel is the fifth generation of the Bechtel family to lead the company. Bechtel serves on the boards of trustees for the National Geographic Society and the Center for Strategic and International Studies, as well as on the board of directors for the Business Roundtable. He serves on the board of advisors for the Fremont Group and is a member of the American Society of Corporate Executives. Bechtel graduated with a BA in geography from Middlebury College and an MBA and an MSE in construction engineering and management from Stanford University.

Charles Boustany Jr. is a partner at Capitol Counsel, LLC, and counselor at the National Bureau of Asian Research, where he co-chaired the Task Force on Transforming the Economic Dimension of U.S. China Strategy. Boustany is a former U.S. representative (R-LA) who served as a subcommittee chairman on the House Committee on Ways and Means. In Congress, Boustany was a leader on trade policy, foreign economic policy, and international taxation. He co-chaired the bipartisan U.S.-China Working Group in the House of Representatives and led congressional delegations to China. As a member of the House Democracy Partnership, he conducted seminars on congressional oversight for members of parliament from emerging democracies. Prior to serving in Congress, Boustany practiced medicine in the field of thoracic and cardiovascular surgery. He is currently serving a two-year term as president of the U.S. Association of Former Members of Congress and is a member of the National Committee on U.S.-China Relations. Boustany received a doctorate in medicine from Louisiana State University.

L. Reginald Brothers Jr. is the chief executive officer of NuWave Solutions. Most recently, Brothers was the chief technology officer of Peraton, and, prior to that, he was a principal with the Chertoff Group. From 2014 to 2017, he served as undersecretary for science and technology at the U.S. Department of Homeland Security (DHS), where he was responsible for a science and technology portfolio that included basic and applied research, development, demonstration, testing, and evaluation, to help DHS operational elements and the nation's first responders achieve their mission objectives. From 2011 to 2014, Brothers served as deputy assistant secretary of defense for research at the Department of Defense. In this position, he was responsible for policy and oversight of the department's science and technology programs and laboratories. He has held senior roles at the Defense Advanced Research Projects Agency, BAE Systems, Draper Laboratory, and the Massachusetts Institute of Technology's Lincoln Laboratory. Brothers received a BS in electrical engineering from Tufts University, an MS in electrical engineering from Southern Methodist University, and a PhD in electrical engineering and computer science from the Massachusetts Institute of Technology.

Joyce Chang is chair of global research for JPMorgan's Corporate and Investment Bank, a global leader in banking, markets and investor services. JPMorgan's global research professionals study all sectors in which the firm does business, including equities, fixed income, currency and commodities, emerging markets, derivatives, and structured finance. The global research team was named *Institutional Investor's* Top Global Research Firm for 2017 and 2018. Chang began her career as an emerging markets strategist and held top rankings in *Institutional Investor* surveys for emerging markets research from 1997 through 2012, earning twenty-five number-one individual rankings. In 2014, she was inducted into the Fixed Income Analyst Society's hall of fame. Chang was a managing director at Merrill Lynch and Salomon Brothers before joining JPMorgan Chase in 1999. She is the senior sponsor for JPMorgan's corporate and investment bank Women on the Move network, the Asian and Pacific Islanders Reaching for Excellence network (AsPIRE), and the nonprofit board service.

Evan A. Feigenbaum is vice president for studies at the Carnegie Endowment for International Peace. He was also the 2019–20 James R. Schlesinger distinguished professor at the University of Virginia's Miller Center of Public Affairs, where he is now a practitioner senior fellow. Initially an academic, his career has spanned government service, think tanks, the private sector, and three regions of Asia. From 2001 to 2009, he served at the U.S. State Department as deputy assistant secretary of state for South Asia (2007–2009), deputy assistant secretary of state for Central Asia (2006–2007), member of the policy planning staff with principal responsibility for East Asia and the Pacific (2001–2006), and an advisor on China to Deputy Secretary of State Robert B. Zoellick. He is the author of three books and monographs, including *The United States in the New Asia and China's Techno-Warriors: National Security and Strategic Competition from the Nuclear to the Information Age,* as well as numerous articles and essays. He earned his PhD in Chinese politics from Stanford University.

Jennifer Hillman is a senior fellow at the Council on Foreign Relations and a professor at the Georgetown University Law Center. In 2012, she completed her term as one of seven members serving on the World Trade Organization (WTO)'s highest court, its Appellate Body. As a commissioner at the U.S. International

Trade Commission, she adjudicated trade remedy cases along with conducting trade-related economic studies. Through her work as general counsel at the Office of the U.S. Trade Representative (USTR), Hillman was involved in all litigation matters coming before panels of the North American Free Trade Agreement or the WTO. She negotiated bilateral agreements with forty-five countries while serving as the USTR's ambassador and chief textiles negotiator. Before joining the USTR, she was the legislative director for Senator Terry Sanford (D-NC). Hillman was a partner in the law firm Cassidy Levy Kent, a senior transatlantic fellow for the German Marshall Fund of the United States, and a member of the selection panel for the Harry Truman Scholarship Foundation. She serves on the board of visitors of Duke University's Sanford School of Public Policy. She is a graduate of Duke University and Harvard Law School.

Christopher M. Kirchhoff is a senior fellow at Schmidt Futures. During the Barack Obama administration, Kirchhoff served as an aide to the chairman of the Joint Chiefs of Staff, advisor to presidential counselor John Podesta, and director for strategic planning for the National Security Council. He led both the chairman's initiatives team and the National Security Council's strategic planning small group, working on issues ranging from how technology will change the future of security to Operation United Assistance, which deployed three thousand U.S. service members to end the Ebola epidemic in West Africa. Kirchhoff also helped create and lead Defense Innovation Unit X, the Pentagon's Silicon Valley office. Kirchhoff began his career on the staff of the space shuttle *Columbia* accident investigation and went on to write the U.S. government history *Hard Lessons: The Iraq Reconstruction Experience,* coined "The Iraq Pentagon Papers" by the *New York Times.* He has been awarded the Civilian Service Medal for hazardous duty in Iraq and the Secretary of Defense Medal for Outstanding Service. From 2011 to 2015, he was the highest-ranking openly gay advisor in the U.S. military. Kirchhoff graduated from Harvard College and holds a doctorate in politics from Cambridge University, where he was a Gates Scholar.

Jacob J. Lew served as the seventy-sixth U.S. secretary of the treasury from 2013 to 2017. Previously, he served as White House chief of staff to President Barack Obama and director of the Office of Management and Budget in both the Obama and Clinton administrations. He has also served as deputy secretary of state and as principal domestic policy advisor to House Speaker Thomas P. O'Neill Jr., in addition to holding a variety of private sector and nonprofit roles. Lew is a managing partner at Lindsay Goldberg and a member of the faculty at Columbia University's School of International and Public Affairs.

Natalie Lichtenstein was the inaugural general counsel at the Asian Infrastructure Investment Bank (AIIB) and chief counsel for AIIB's establishment from 2014 to 2016. She played a crucial role as the legal architect for this new international organization. She retired in 2010 from a thirty-year legal career at the World Bank, where she worked on lending operations in China and other countries and institutional governance. She served as chief counsel for East Asia and assistant general counsel for institutional affairs, and led the staff team supporting the 2010 shareholding and governance reforms. Before joining the World Bank in 1980, she was an attorney-advisor at the U.S. Department of the Treasury, where she worked on the normalization of U.S.-China relations and U.S. participation in international financial institutions. She taught Chinese law at Johns Hopkins' University's School of Advanced International Studies (SAIS) and elsewhere. She is an SAIS visiting scholar and a member of the advisory board of Duke Kunshan University in China. She is the author of *A Comparative Guide to the Asian Infrastructure Investment Bank.* Lichtenstein received her AB in East Asian studies and her JD from Harvard University.

Gary Locke is the interim president of Bellevue College, which is the third-largest higher education institution in Washington State, serving nearly thirty thousand students annually. As Washington State's twenty-first governor from 1997 to 2005—the nation's most trade-dependent state—Locke increased exports of Washington products and services by leading trade missions to Mexico, Asia, and Europe, more than doubling the state's exports to China. As secretary of commerce from 2009 to 2011, he led President Barack Obama's National Export Initiative to double U.S. exports; assumed a troubled 2010 census process under which his active supervision ended on time and $2 billion under budget; and achieved the most significant reduction in patent application processing in the agency's history, from forty months down to twelve. As ambassador to China from 2011 to 2014, he opened markets for U.S. goods and services; reduced wait times for visa interviews of Chinese applicants from one hundred days to three days; and through the embassy's air quality monitoring program, exposed the severity of air pollution in China, leading to the Chinese people demand action by their government.

Oriana Skylar Mastro is a center fellow at the Freeman Spogli Institute for International Studies at Stanford University, where her research focuses on Chinese military and security policy, Asia-Pacific security issues, war termination, and coercive diplomacy. She is also nonresident senior fellow at the American Enterprise Institute and continues to serve in the U.S. Air Force Reserve, for which she works as a strategic planner at the U.S. Indo-Pacific Command's Strategy and Assessments Division. For her contributions to U.S. strategy in Asia, she won the Individual Reservist of the Year Award in 2016. She has published widely, including in *Asian Security, Foreign Affairs, International Security, International Studies Review, Journal of Strategic Studies, National Interest, Survival,* and *Washington Quarterly.* Her book, *The Costs of Conversation: Obstacles to Peace Talks in Wartime,* won the 2020 American Political Science Association's Best Book by an Untenured Faculty Member in the International Security Section. She holds a BA in East Asian studies from Stanford University and an MA and PhD in politics from Princeton University.

Daniel H. Rosen is a founding partner of the Rhodium Group and leads the firm's work on China and the world economy. Rosen's focus includes U.S.-China policy dynamics, interpretation of Chinese economic performance indicators, and assessment of long-term Chinese reform and policy directions. Rhodium's China research contributes to corporate strategy and planning, investment management, and political risk assessment of China and its global interactions. Rosen is an adjunct associate professor at Columbia University, where he has taught a graduate seminar on the Chinese economy at the School of International and Public Affairs since 2001. From 2000 to 2001, Rosen was senior advisor for international economic policy at the White House National Economic Council and National Security Council, where he played a crucial role in completing China's accession to the World Trade Organization and accompanied President Bill Clinton to Asia for summits and state visits. He is affiliated with a number of preeminent U.S. think tanks focused on international economics. Since 1992, he has authored more than a dozen books and reports on aspects of China's economic and commercial development. Rosen serves on the board of the National Committee on U.S.-China Relations.

Gary Roughead is the Robert and Marion Oster distinguished military fellow at the Hoover Institution at Stanford University. Previously, he served as the twenty-ninth chief of naval operations after holding six operational commands. He is one of only two officers in the history of the navy to have commanded both the U.S. Atlantic and Pacific fleets. Ashore, he served as the commandant of the U.S. Naval Academy, where he led the strategic planning effort that underpinned that institution's first capital campaign. He was the navy's chief of legislative affairs, responsible for the Department of the Navy's interaction with Congress. Roughead was also the deputy commander of the U.S. Pacific Command. He serves on the boards of directors of the Northrop Grumman Corporation; Maersk Line, Limited; and the Marinette Marine Corporation. He is a trustee of the Dodge and Cox Funds and Johns Hopkins University and serves on the board of managers of Johns Hopkins University's Applied Physics Laboratory. He is a graduate of the U.S. Naval Academy.

David Sacks is a research fellow at the Council on Foreign Relations, where his work focuses on U.S.-China relations, U.S.-Taiwan relations, Chinese foreign policy, cross-Strait relations, and the political thought of Hans Morgenthau. He was previously the special assistant to the president for research at the Council on Foreign Relations (CFR). Prior to joining CFR, Sacks worked on political military affairs at the American Institute in Taiwan, which handles the full breadth of the United States' relationship with Taiwan in the absence of diplomatic ties. Sacks was also a Princeton in Asia fellow in Hangzhou, China. Sacks received his BA in political science from Carleton College and his MA in international relations and international economics from Johns Hopkins University's School of Advanced International Studies. At SAIS, he was the recipient of the A. Doak Barnett Award, given annually to the most distinguished China Studies graduate.

Nadia Schadlow is a senior fellow at the Hudson Institute. She was most recently the U.S. deputy national security advisor for strategy. Prior to joining the National Security Council, she was a senior program officer in the Smith Richardson Foundation's international security and foreign policy program, where she helped identify strategic issues that warrant further attention from the U.S. policy community. She served on the Defense Policy Board from 2006 to 2009. Her articles have appeared in *American Interest, Parameters, Philanthropy, Wall Street Journal,* and several edited volumes. Schadlow holds a BA in government and Soviet studies from Cornell University and MA and PhD from Johns Hopkins University's School of Advanced International Studies.

Rajiv J. Shah serves as president of the Rockefeller Foundation, a global institution with a mission to promote the well-being of humanity around the world. The foundation applies data, science, and innovation to improve health for all, nourish the world, end energy poverty, and enable meaningful economic mobility. In 2009, Shah was appointed U.S. Agency for International Development administrator by President Obama, where he led the U.S. response to the Haiti earthquake and the West African Ebola pandemic. Previously, he served at the Bill & Melinda Gates Foundation, where he created the International Finance Facility for Immunization, which helped reshape the global vaccine industry and save millions of lives.

Kristen Silverberg is executive vice president for policy at Business Roundtable, where she leads the policy team. She previously served as a managing director at the Institute of International Finance. She served in the George W. Bush administration as U.S. ambassador to the European Union and as assistant secretary of state for international organization affairs. Prior to her time at the State Department, she held a number of senior positions at the White House, including deputy domestic policy advisor. Silverberg served in Baghdad, Iraq, for which she received the Secretary of Defense Medal for Outstanding Public Service. She formerly practiced law at Williams and Connolly, LLP, in Washington, DC, and served as a law clerk to Supreme Court Justice Clarence Thomas and U.S. Court of Appeals Judge David Sentelle. Silverberg serves on the board of directors of the CDC Foundation, the International Republican Institute, and Vorbeck Materials, as well as the advisory board of the *Texas National Security Review* and the national advisory council of the Aspen Institute's Future of Work Initiative. She was recognized by the World Economic Forum as a Young Global Leader. She attended Harvard College and the University of Texas School of Law.

Taiya M. Smith is senior fellow for global impact at the Climate Leadership Council and a nonresident senior associate at the Center for Strategic and International Studies. Smith is also the cofounder of Phylleos, Inc. Previously, as managing partner at Garnet Strategies, Smith advised multinational companies, financial institutions, and trade associations on climate and energy policy, U.S.-China relations, geopolitical risk, and matters arising in global forums. Serving as deputy chief of staff and executive secretary to Treasury Secretary Hank Paulson, Smith led the U.S-China Strategic Economic Dialogue, managed the U.S. negotiating team, and established the U.S.-China Ten Year Framework on Energy and the Environment and the EcoPartnership program. Smith served as special assistant to Deputy Secretary of State Robert B. Zoellick advising on Africa, Europe, and political and military affairs. Prior to that, Smith was the State Department's point person on Darfur, spending much of her time in Darfur working with international donors, the Sudanese government, and rebel factions. Prior to joining the government, she served as a member of the facilitation team for the Burundi Peace Negotiations led by Nelson Mandela. Smith holds a BA from Wesleyan University and a MPP from the Harvard Kennedy School of Government.

Susan A. Thornton is visiting lecturer in law at Yale Law School and senior fellow at Yale Law School's Paul Tsai China Center. In 2018, she retired from the U.S. State Department after a twenty-eight–year diplomatic career focused primarily on East and Central Asia. In leadership roles in Washington, Thornton worked on China and Korea policy, including stabilizing relations with Taiwan, the U.S.-China Cyber Agreement, and the Paris climate accord. She led a successful negotiation in Pyongyang for monitoring the Agreed Framework on denuclearization. In her eighteen years of overseas postings in China, Russia, the Caucasus, and Central Asia, Thornton's leadership furthered U.S. interests and influence and maintained programs and mission morale in a host of difficult operating environments. Prior to joining the Foreign Service, she was among the first State Department Reagan-Fascell Democracy fellows and served from 1989 to 1990 at the U.S. Consulate in Leningrad. She was also a researcher at the Foreign Policy Institute from 1987 to 1991. She is on the board of trustees for the Eurasia Foundation. Thornton holds degrees from the National Defense University's Eisenhower School, Johns Hopkins University's School of Advanced International Studies, and Bowdoin College.

Ramin Toloui is professor of the practice of international finance at Stanford University and the Tad and Dianne Taube policy fellow at the Stanford Institute for Economic Policy Research. His teaching and research focus on international economic policy, financial crises, and the economic impact of artificial intelligence. He served as assistant secretary for international finance at the U.S. Treasury Department in the Obama administration and previously managed $100 billion in assets as global cohead of emerging markets at PIMCO. He holds a bachelor's degree in economics from Harvard University and master's degree in international relations from Oxford University, where he was a Rhodes Scholar.

Macani Toungara has more than fourteen of years of international economic development and management consulting experience in the private and nonprofit sectors. At the time of the Task Force deliberations, she was manager of international programs in Africa for the Obama Foundation. In this role, she managed the foundation's programming across the African continent. The flagship program, Leaders: Africa, inspires, empowers, and connects two hundred emerging African leaders through a year-long program of capacity-building. Previously, Toungara was senior director for program development at TechnoServe, where she managed the development of strategic bids and led donor engagement with the Bill & Melinda Gates Foundation, the U.S. Department of Agriculture, and the United Kingdom's Department for International Development. She has expertise on subjects including public-private partnerships, supply chain linkages, small- and medium-sized enterprise (SME) development, market systems development, food security promotion, and job creation. Before joining TechnoServe, Toungara was a consultant with the Boston Consulting Group, where she worked on projects in consumer goods and financial services. She holds a BA in economics from Harvard University, an MPA from

Princeton University's School of Public and International Affairs, and a JD from the Georgetown University Law Center.

Frederick H. Tsai is the vice president and head of global customer success at Liferay, a growth stage enterprise software company headquartered in Los Angeles. At Liferay, he leads the teams and programs responsible for customer engagement, adoption, and retention. He is also founder and head of the Young China Watchers of San Francisco. Previously, he was senior director of strategy at Salesforce. Prior to that, Tsai spent nearly ten years living and working in Asia, where he served in senior roles at Dell, including as director of China strategy. Tsai began his career in technology investment banking at Deutsche Bank in San Francisco. He graduated from Washington University in St. Louis and received his MA in international relations from Johns Hopkins University's School of Advanced International Studies.

TASK FORCE OBSERVERS

Observers participate in Task Force discussions but are not asked to join the consensus. They participate in their individual, not institutional, capacities.

Paul J. Angelo is a fellow for Latin America studies at the Council on Foreign Relations. His work focuses on U.S.-Latin America relations, transnational crime, violent actors, military and police reform, and immigration. A former active-duty naval officer, Angelo has extensive experience in military and government service. He served as a political officer at the U.S. Embassy in Tegucigalpa, Honduras, where he managed the ambassador's security and justice portfolio. His previous service in the U.S. Navy included tours at the U.S. Embassy in Bogota, Colombia; in a United Kingdom–based North Atlantic Treaty Organization position; onboard a destroyer deployed to the Asia-Pacific region; and as an instructor at the U.S. Naval Academy, where he taught Spanish language and Latin American politics courses. Angelo holds a BS in political science from the U.S. Naval Academy, where he was awarded the Harry S. Truman Scholarship; an MPhil in Latin American studies from the University of Oxford, where he studied as a Rhodes Scholar; and a PhD in politics from University College London.

Alyssa Ayres is adjunct senior fellow for India, Pakistan, and South Asia at the Council on Foreign Relations. She is also dean of George Washington University's Elliott School of International Affairs. She is a foreign policy practitioner and award-winning author with senior experience in the government, nonprofit, and private sectors. She is also interested in the emergence of subnational participation in foreign policy, particularly the growth of international city networks. Ayres came to CFR after serving as deputy assistant secretary of state for South Asia from 2010 to 2013. Before serving in the Barack Obama administration, Ayres was founding director of the India and South Asia practice at McLarty Associates, the Washington-based international strategic advisory firm, from 2008 to 2010. Her book about India's rise on the world stage, *Our Time Has Come: How India Is Making Its Place in the World,* was selected by the *Financial Times* for its Summer 2018: Politics list, and she is working on a new book project about India's urban transformation. She received an AB from Harvard College and an MA and PhD from the University of Chicago.

Robert C. Francis Jr., a captain in the U.S. Navy, commanded the navy destroyer USS *Lassen,* making multiple patrols to the East and South China Seas. He has also served in multiple aircraft carriers and guided missile frigates conducting counternarcotics, counter-piracy, freedom of navigation operations, and multiple Operation Enduring Freedom and Operation Iraqi Freedom missions. His staff assignments include military assistant to the assistant secretary of defense for Indo-Pacific security affairs and the assistant readiness officer on the Commander Naval Surface Force, U.S. Pacific Fleet staff. Francis earned a BA in physics from the University of San Diego, an MBA from National University, and an MS in engineering management from Old Dominion University.

Michelle D. Gavin is senior fellow for Africa Studies at the Council on Foreign Relations. She has more than twenty years of experience in international affairs in government and nonprofit roles. She was formerly the managing director of the Africa Center, a multidisciplinary institution dedicated to increasing understanding of contemporary Africa. From 2011 to 2014, she was the U.S. ambassador to Botswana and served concurrently as the U.S. representative to the Southern African Development Community (SADC). Prior to that, Gavin was a special assistant to President Obama and the senior director for Africa at the National Security Council. Before joining the Obama administration, she was an international affairs fellow and adjunct fellow for Africa at CFR. Earlier in her career, she worked in the U.S. Senate, where she was the staff director for the Senate Foreign Relations Committee's Subcommittee on African Affairs, director of international policy issues for Senator Russ Feingold (D-WI), and legislative director for Senator Ken Salazar (D-CO).

Joshua Kurlantzick is senior fellow for Southeast Asia at the Council on Foreign Relations. He was previously a visiting scholar at the Carnegie Endowment for International Peace, where he studied Southeast Asian politics and economics and China's relations with Southeast Asia, including Chinese investment, aid, and diplomacy. Previously, he was a fellow at the University of Southern California's Center on Public Diplomacy and a fellow at the Pacific Council on International Policy. Kurlantzick focuses on China's relations with Southeast Asia and China's approach to soft power, including state-backed media and information efforts and other components of soft power. He is also working on issues related to the rise of global populism and, particularly, populism in Asia. He is completing a new book on China's information and influence activities around the world. Kurlantzick received his BA in political science from Haverford College.

Mira Rapp-Hooper was previously the Stephen A. Schwarzman senior fellow for Asia studies at the Council on Foreign Relations. She was also a senior fellow at Yale Law School's Paul Tsai China Center. At CFR, Rapp-Hooper's work explored national security and strategy issues in Asia, including great power competition, alliances, nuclear issues, and territorial disputes; the implications of China's rise for the international order; and the future of U.S. strategy toward Asia and China. She is the author of two books, *Shields of the Republic: The Triumph and Peril of America's Alliances,* and *An Open World: How America Can Win the Contest for Twenty-First-Century Order,* coauthored with Rebecca Lissner. She holds a BA in history from Stanford University and an MA, MPhil, and PhD in political science from Columbia University.

Anya Schmemann (ex officio) is Washington director of global communications and outreach and director of the Independent Task Force Program at the Council on Foreign Relations in Washington, DC. At CFR, Schmemann has overseen numerous high-level Task Forces on a wide range of topics, including pandemic preparedness, innovation, the future of work, Arctic strategy, nuclear weapons, climate change, immigration, trade policy, and internet governance, as well as on U.S. policy toward Afghanistan, Brazil, North Korea, Pakistan, and Turkey. She previously served as assistant dean for communications and outreach at American University's School of International Service and managed communications at Harvard Kennedy School's Belfer Center for Science and International Affairs, where she also administered the Caspian studies program. She coordinated a research project on Russian security issues at the EastWest Institute in New York and was assistant director of CFR's Center for Preventive Action in New York, focusing on the Balkans and Central Asia. She was a Truman National Security Fellow and is co-chair of the Global Kids DC advisory council. Schmemann received a BA in government and an MA in Russian studies from Harvard University.

Benn Steil is senior fellow and director of international economics, as well as the official historian in residence, at the Council on Foreign Relations in New York. He is also founding editor of *International Finance,* a scholarly economics journal. Prior to joining CFR in 1999, he was director of the International Economics Programme at the Royal Institute of International Affairs in London. He came to the institute in 1992 from a Lloyd's of London Tercentenary Research Fellowship at University of Oxford University's Nuffield College. Steil is lead writer of CFR's *Geo-Graphics* economics blog; creator of the web-based interactives "Global Monetary Policy Tracker," "Global Imbalances Tracker," "Sovereign Risk Tracker," "Central Bank Currency Swap Tracker," "Belt and Road Tracker," and "Global Growth Tracker"; and the author, most recently, of *The Marshall Plan: Dawn of the Cold War* and *The Battle of Bretton Woods: John Maynard Keynes, Harry Dexter White, and the Making of a New World Order*. He holds a BSc in economics from the University of Pennsylvania's Wharton School and an MPhil and DPhil in economics from Oxford University's Nuffield College.

Jennifer Hendrixson White served as a senior professional staff member for the House Committee on Foreign Affairs at the time of the Task Force deliberations. In this role she was the principal advisor to the chairman and Democratic members on matters relating to East Asia and the Pacific and institutional oversight of the State Department and the U.S. Agency for International Development. Prior to joining the committee, White was coordinator of the Department of State's U.S.-China Strategic Economic Dialogue and previously held positions with the Asia Pacific Economic Cooperation (APEC), the East Asia Summit (EAS), and the Association of Southeast Asian Nations (ASEAN). Before joining government, she worked on financial inclusion at the World Bank and worked in China, Myanmar, and Thailand, where she managed programs related to development and human security.

Contributing CFR Staff

Dalia Albarrán
Senior Graphic Designer,
Product and Design

Sabine Baumgartner
Senior Photo Editor,
Product and Design

Michael Bricknell
Data Visualization Designer,
Product and Design

Natalia Cote-Muñoz
Research Associate,
Latin America Studies

Kirk Lancaster
Research Associate, Asia Studies

Patricia Lee Dorff
Editorial Director, Publishing

Will Merrow
Data Visualization Designer,
Product and Design

Chloe Moffett
Senior Editor, Publishing

Sarah Perrin
Communications Associate,
Foreign Affairs

Anya Schmemann
Director, Independent
Task Force Program

Chelie Setzer
Associate Director, Independent
Task Force Program

Sara Shah
Program Associate, Washington
Meetings and Independent Task
Force Program

Alex Tippett
Research Associate,
International Economics

Katherine Vidal
Deputy Design Director,
Product and Design

Christian Wolan
Senior Product Manager,
Product and Design

Contributing Interns

Isaac Gershberg
Geoeconomic Studies

Camilla He
Independent Task Force Program

Callie McQuilkin
Independent Task Force Program

Allison Pluemer
Independent Task Force Program

Michael Rubin
Asia Studies

Dominic Solari
Independent Task Force Program